Southern Deer & Deer Hunting

by Larry Weishuhn & Bill Bynum

Published by

 **krause publications**

700 E. State Street • Iola, WI 54990-0001

Please call or write for our free catalog of outdoor publications. Our toll-free number to
place an order or obtain a free catalog is 800-258-0929 or please use our regular business
telephone 715-445-2214 for editorial comment
and further information.

Library of Congress Catalog Number: 95-77306
ISBN: 0-87341-335-0
Printed in the United States of America

Contents

Dedication

This book is in loving dedication to my favorite hunting partner and friend, William Harold Bynum. Together we have explored the world of the white-tailed deer. Many of our explorations will remain as cherished memories for all my life, memories that only a father and son can share. I would also like to acknowledge James "Pappy" Holt who taught me many of nature's secrets.

Bill Bynum

Dedication

To my wife Mary Anne, daughters Beth and Theresa, who have for many years put up with my being gone during the fall, and my wishing it was already fall in the spring and summer. To my parents, Lester and Lillie Weishuhn, who during my formative years gave me a life in the out-of-doors. To A.J. and Tillie Aschenbeck, my maternal grandparents who encouraged and taught a freckle-faced, red-haired lad to appreciate the woods and fields. To the many friends with whom I have shared time in deer camps, especially my brother Glenn, and old friends such as Ron Porter, J. Wayne and Sherry Fears and many, many others, may their "kind" and white-tailed deer always remain!

Larry Weishuhn

Foreword

I consider myself one of the most fortunate deer hunters in the country. I have had the opportunity to hunt with two of the best deer hunters and outdoorsmen around, Larry Weishuhn and Bill Bynum. Not only are these two gentlemen fun to share a remote campfire with, but each hunt with them is like an advanced course in the art and science of deer hunting. Fortunately for all deer hunters, they came out of the woods long enough to write this book.

Getting to know Larry Weishuhn came about due to our mutual interest in managing white-tailed deer. Back in the early 1980s, I kept hearing about a white-tailed deer biologist in Texas who had an uncanny knowledge about these animals. I sought out this deer guru and we became friends by telephone. He invited my wife and me to hunt with him on a ranch where he was running a deer management program in south Texas. We jumped at the chance to hunt with him.

We arrived at the ranch to find Weishuhn running a one-man hunting operation. With six hunters in camp, he was the cook, guide, game processor, and mechanic. What most impressed my wife and me about this one-man outfitting service was that he was good at all the tasks, made it look easy, and kept smiling even though he was getting only two hours of sleep each night. I knew at once this was a unique outdoorsman.

Since that first meeting we have shared speaking platforms, cold camps, canteens, pots of beans, deer management information, mountaintops, and a white, one-eyed mule. He knows whitetail behavior as no one I have ever known. This, plus his outstanding whitetail hunting skills, led me to write an article several years ago in which I called him "Mr. Whitetail." The name stuck, and rightfully so.

Bill Bynum and I go back far enough that neither of us cares to discuss it. As Weishuhn can read the innards of a deer, Bynum can read the woods. I was once writing an introduction for Bynum that I was to give at one of the NRA Great American Hunting Tour appearances. As I tried to sum up Bynum in one word, "woodsman" kept coming to mind.

If there is a Daniel Boone among us in this last decade of the 20th century, it's Bill Bynum. He is a master deer hunter with bow, muzzleloader, or modern firearm. He can discuss fishing, trapping, predator calling, or camping skills with the authority that only comes from one who has been there many times. I have been on deer hunts, predator calling trips, and beaver trapping expeditions with him. Each time I have found myself saying over and over, "Why didn't I think of that?"

To get these two giants of the outdoor world together to pool their knowledge of deer hunting is a gift to you, the reader of this book. Like me, you can now go hunting with these two woods-wise wizards and throughout the book you will catch yourself saying, "Why didn't I think of that?"

So put another log on the fire, prop up your feet, and join Larry and Bill on the deer hunts found throughout this book. When you finish the last page, like me, you will be fortunate to have hunted with these two experts.

- J. Wayne Fears

Chapter 1

Southern Traditions of Hunting Deer

Larry L. Weishuhn

Opening day had finally become more than simply a promise. Tomorrow would be *the* day. For the past weeks the family, my dad, mother, brother, grandmother, and I had been preparing our deer camp, stocking it with food, chopping firewood for the old cast iron stove and generally getting things in order for the upcoming hunting season and spending several days in deer camp. For the past two months we had been checking deer trails, looking for rubs and scrapes and scouting at every opportunity, as well as repositioning our old deer stands and setting up new ones. When all this was taken care of, we made sure our shotguns and rifles were properly sighted in. All was ready.

The night before opening day several families and other hunters in our community left their own camps to join us at our's, for the annual hunter's stew. Each year it became the "duty" of another camp to host the event the night before the season opened. By the time we sat down for supper there were nearly 40 people. Camp was alive with activity. Old-timers told of hunting back when they drove teams of horse-drawn wagons to where they would camp for several weeks each fall. Others told of the slim times when seeing even a deer track caused quite a stir in our little Germanic community of Zimmerscheidt, just north of Cummins Creek in the western part of southeast Texas. All around hunters argued about which was the best deer rifle, or what was the best buckshot load for shotguns.

Times were changing in the late 1950s. Our area was finally once again starting to support a few whitetails. Deer had come on hard times back during the late 1800s and during the hungry days of the early 1900s, and especially during the Great Depression. During World War II deer started returning, only to be devastated by outbreaks of screwworms, a pesky flesh-eating fly larvae that extracted a heavy toll from the area's wildlife.

As a youngster growing up in rural Texas, during the early and mid-1950s, I spent many hours looking for deer throughout the year. The sight of one was a real treat, regardless of the season. Deer were present in our area, but not in great numbers. However, by the early 1960s things started changing. The screwworm was practically eradicated, the habitat had started changing and improving, and the deer responded. Whitetails in our area increased to a new high. Many areas of the South were experiencing similar increases.

Newly developed game management techniques included trapping and transplanting large numbers of deer into areas where years before the whitetail had practically been removed due to market hunting, subsistence hunting, and primarily changes in wildlife habitat. This increase in deer populations with only local exceptions has continued through the mid-1990s.

The South has long been known for its abundant wildlife. The area has also produced some of the most well-known hunters in American history including such notables as Davy Crockett, Daniel Boone and many, many others. Throughout the early years of exploration, adventurers and hunters played an important role in settling the southern regions of the modern day United States. Early hunters were portrayed as buckskin clad adventurers, in search of new lands to hunt. They led the way and settlements soon followed.

American Indians and the explorers of the early North American continent relied heavily upon deer and other game, not only for food but also for clothing and other necessities of life. Early travelers and explorers told of Indians driving deer and taking them in great numbers. Paintings based on journals written by the early travelers through the area depict Indian and

The sight of deer tracks brings about excitement in a Southern hunter.

Anglo hunters using torches to spot a deer's eyes at night, making them somewhat easier to take. Deer were hunted out of necessity, and not simply for the pure joy of hunting. However, I believe some of the early settlers in the area would have tended to disagree. I strongly suspect many of the earlier warriors, explorers, and settlers of the South greatly enjoyed the "task" of hunting deer and other animals for food, and the enjoyment went considerably farther than simply food gathering.

A Change To Sports Hunting

The early 1900s saw the emergence of the gentleman hunter, who hunted for sport as well as food. Most hunted on their own plantation lands. Those who did not have property joined others who did. Hunting clubs were just starting to emerge in the South. Gentrified landowners, and plantation owners, invited friends and family to join them for hunts on their properties. Much of the hunting that took place during the first half of this century was done with a variety of dogs and hounds. Nowhere else in North America was dog hunting for white-tailed deer more widespread or more popular. Lines of hounds and dogs were bred, developed, and trained specifically to chase deer.

Much of the South, which had once been forest, then cleared for the times of "King Cotton," slowly started reforesting, making for thick, almost impenetrable tangles of trees, vines, and underbrush. Deer were still relatively scarce. It became almost a necessity to use dogs to trail and drive deer from thickets. Hunters stationed themselves along known crossings and trails with rifles and shotguns in hopes of getting a fleeting shot at a deer. Large plantations throughout the South hosted a limited number of such hunts and hunters. A tradition of hunting deer with hounds was born. Perhaps this was much more of a rebirth, since many of the early explorers and hunters used dogs to hunt deer and other game such as black bear.

Some of the deer-dog hunters hunted to take a deer, others simply loved to listen to the "mountain music" created by dogs and hounds "chopping and bawling" as they chased deer. Volumes have been written about these types of deer hunts. Authors such as Archibald Rutledge and many others extolled the virtues of the deer they hunted, the hounds that pursued them, and the hunters and their aides who followed the hounds.

This way of hunting deer survived for many years, and still continues in some areas. While some do not approve of hunting deer with hounds, it is nonetheless a traditional way to hunt deer in the South.

As someone who grew up hunting small game with hounds, albeit used for chasing raccoons and fox, I truly enjoy the sounds made by a pack of well-trained dogs pursuing their quarry. In my dad's pack of hounds, if a dog chased deer, he was either broken of the habit or he found a new home. As a biologist who has long been involved with quality deer management and hunting, I understand the "feelings" some hunters have against dog hunting. I also do not necessarily approve of such hunting practices. But I am not one who quickly condemns those who use dogs to hunt deer. I realize times are changing and many folks these days do not approve of hunting deer in this manner. However, I do feel a bit of sadness when Southerners are no longer allowed to use dogs to chase and hunt deer, as we are losing a great Southern tradition. Deer hunting in general will lose a portion of its tradition as well.

Even if you oppose hunting deer with dogs, there has got to be some excitement upon hearing a pack of dogs seemingly chasing a deer your way. While hunting in southwestern Georgia recently, sitting high in a tree stand overlooking a brushy creek bottom, I heard the barking of several dogs in the distance. It sounded as if they were coming my way. The sounds made by the dogs were barely audible when I heard a deer running my way. My excitement increased dramatically as I anticipated a huge buck stepping out of the brambles and briars. Instead I watched a doe run through the edge of the thicket. She stopped and looked in the direction that the ruckus was coming from. Content they were still a long way behind, she slowly crossed the creek and disappeared into the opposite thicket. The sound of the dogs came closer. Fifteen minutes later they came near my stand. Five dachshunds slowly worked the trail the doe had taken. Somehow I doubted seriously they would be catching up with her. I suspect for the deer, that was certainly a fair chase!

Most of the hunters who hunted deer in the South with dogs, preferred dogs that were slow in following the track of a deer, rather than pushing them hard. Such dogs did not chase deer completely out of the country, but simply moved them, thereby giving hunters a much better chance of a shot.

As a youngster, I knew several who hunted deer with dogs in eastern Texas, Mississippi, Alabama, and Arkansas. At the time I raised beagles, my dad, brother, and I used them to hunt cottontails and swamp rabbits. Several of the puppies my dogs produced were bought by these gentlemen to hunt deer. According to them, the slower trailing dogs were far superior to larger hounds that tended to push the deer too hard. It must have been an enjoyable way to hunt the nearly impenetrable thickets, and certainly more productive than still hunting or nearly any other technique.

I have seen what packs of wild dogs can do to a deer herd, especially if the dogs are allowed to freely roam the woods throughout the year. These dogs are considerably different from those used during well-organized dog/deer hunts of yesterday or even today.

Alas, I strongly suspect in the not too distant future we will see a total ban on using dogs to hunt deer. And even though I have never hunted deer in this manner, I will feel a bit of sadness and mourn the loss of a traditional Southern way of hunting deer.

After World War II, more and more hunters started hunting deer and soon hunters started getting together to form hunting clubs. To ensure they would have hunting rights on private and timber properties, they started leasing parcels of lands to gain exclusive hunting rights on those properties. Primarily these were hunters who did not wish to compete with other hunters on public lands, even though such properties were abundant in many areas of the South.

With the approach of the middle third of the 1900s, deer became plentiful and game regulations and bag limits were lenient. Bag limits approached a deer a day in some states (and remains so even today). In other states they were not quite so liberal. Nonetheless, if someone really wanted to pursue deer, he could shoot a considerable number over the period of the fall season.

In many areas of the South the measure of success of a Southern deer hunter's season was measured in the number of bucks the hunter bagged each fall. Little thought was given to the size of the deer's rack or his body. Hunters thought primarily in terms of number of deer taken, rather than in the quality. Few if any does were taken. Most hunters considered it sacrilegious to shoot a doe or even talk about shooting does. It was not until the late 1960s or 1970s that hunters even talked about the necessity of doe harvests.

Hunting Lodge - A New Era Is Born

In recent years more and more hunters throughout the South have joined various hunting clubs, even though there is a lot of public land, both state and federally owned. We have also seen the advent of commercial hunts, sometimes referred to as lodge or package hunts. Commercial hunting lodges have sprung up throughout the South since the middle 1970s. One of the first of these commercial ventures, Alabama's Westervelt Lodge, was begun in the 1970s by J. Wayne Fears. Fears spent time in Texas looking at hunting operations such as the famed YO Ranch in the Texas Hill Country, then combined his own ideas and those from other operations throughout North America to establish Westervelt. Soon others started similar operations. Today whitetail hunts at hunting lodges have become popular ways for residents and non-residents of the South to enjoy Southern whitetail hunting and hospitality at its finest.

During the past 40 years of hunting whitetails throughout North America, I have had the opportunity to hunt numerous hunting lodges throughout the South and Southwest. Some of the more interesting of these type of hunts have taken place in Alabama and Georgia. Many of these lodges were established in recent times; however, some can date their establishment back to the 1920s and even earlier. One such camp's walls I visited were lined with photos of successful hunters with their deer and turkeys. Many of those in the photos were politicians, dignitaries, and movie actors of the time. One camp I visited had numerous photos of baseball players such as Dizzy Dean and others of the old Gashouse Gang. Most of the photos were taken during the 1950s and early 1960s. Those were days when writers such as Robert Ruark and others popularized big game hunting. It's a shame those days ever changed and are now gone.

Hunting from lodges and camps throughout the South is an extremely well-organized "experience." In most instances guests hunt from permanent stands or blinds. These are often assigned or drawn by lot to determine where individual hunters will spend the morning or afternoon. On other hunting lands, areas are designated for use by a particular hunter and he or she uses a climber or ladder stand, set up in a place of his/her choice based upon the sign present. Many hunters also use these climber stands while hunting public lands.

Climber stands have become a relatively new Southern tradition. Nowhere are they more popular than in the South, especially in the Southeast where trees grow straight and tall. Where I grew up in the gravel hills of Texas most often our deer stands were built in trees. They were pretty spartan compared to today's blinds and hunting stands. It was not until much later, in the late 1960s and 1970s that hunters started building elaborate walled blinds or shooting houses, which seem to be popular these days in many different areas of the South.

J. Wayne Fears, wildlife biologist/outdoor writer, was one of the first to introduce commercial deer hunting to many areas of the South. Here he enjoys a cup of hunting camp coffee.

As to climbers, I well remember my first encounter with one. I was hunting on lodge property in south-central Alabama. My host instructed me to follow a dim trail through the early morning darkness to a tree where there was hung a climber stand, only a foot or two off the ground. Up until that time, I had never before hunted from a climbing tree stand, and most certainly I had never attempted to crawl up a tree with one!

It took some doing, but I finally, after several attempts, figured out how to make it "crawl." I soon got into the rhythm of crawling. Before I knew it, I was way up in the tree. There I tied myself to the tree with a safety belt. From that lofty perch I had an excellent view of a nearby overgrown field and several white oak trees, as well as a honeysuckle-covered ridge. I enjoyed a great morning of hunting, saw several does, fawns, and a couple of young bucks that I passed.

Just before noon I realized I was expected back at the trail-head at straight-up 12 o'clock. I nearly panicked when I realized I had mastered crawling up a tree with a climbing tree stand, but had not yet thought of how I was going to get down! For a few moments I considered simply staying in the tree all day long, but then realized sooner or later I would have to come down.

I experienced some anxious minutes as I learned how to maneuver the feet portion of the climber in sync with the seat portion of the climber stand. Finally, I was able to crawl down the tree without any great difficulties. It was considerably less traumatic the second time I hunted from a climber.

Throughout this book my co-author, Bill Bynum, and I will touch on traditional Southern ways of hunting deer. As mentioned, new ways of hunting whitetails in the South are fast becoming part of our traditional ways. These days you can hardly be a true Southern whitetail hunter unless you own one or more climbing stands, and carry at least one or more deer calls hung about your neck. In the western portion of the South, most deer hunters also carry a set of rattling horns, and all are dressed in the newest designer camouflage fashions.

In the Southwest horn rattling has long been a tradition. It was in this area, especially Texas, that horn rattling was popularized. These days horn rattling is becoming a popular whitetail hunting technique throughout North America wherever whitetails range. However the vast majority of those who rattle horns to attract bucks still live in the South and Southwest.

Deer Hunting A Lifestyle

Deer hunting in the South is for many a way of life. It has certainly been that way with me most of my life. Seasons are long, bag limits are fairly liberal, deer are relatively abundant, and deer hunting is part of our Southern culture.

Just because deer are plentiful and bag limits liberal does not mean that everyone who hunts in the South is going to take a deer. As this is being written, I have spent many days hunting throughout Alabama, but I have yet to take a deer in that great state where bag limits are a deer per

16

day. Partly this has been my choice, as I enjoy hunting primarily for mature deer. While I have seen a fair number of does, fawns, and young bucks, I have yet to see a mature buck, even while hunting on some extremely well-managed and popular hunting lodges and lands. However my lack of taking a buck has not detracted from the joys of hunting in this great Southern state, which in several ways I have adopted as a second home. Some of my most enjoyable days afield pursuing deer have been spent hunting with J. Wayne and Sherry Fears on their Cross Creek Hollow, where hunting is limited to only a fortunate few.

Hunting in the South is often a family affair where grandfathers hunt with their sons and grandsons, or granddaughters on the same property they hunted with their fathers and grandfathers. Crossings and old tree

Beth Weishuhn started hunting with her father at an early age. In the South families often hunt together.

Southern hunting camps are gathering places for old friends.
Johnnie Hudman, under western hat, and Anthony Ellis enjoy a
campfire and a story.

stands provide great memories. Such is the case on my little place in the gravel hills of Texas. Under a huge old live oak tree sits a hunting camp my family built many years ago. It replaced a camp that my ancestors had used to hunt deer. There also I have found Indian artifacts that indicate the spot was used as a hunting camp long before white men set foot on this continent. All this sits on property that was first purchased by my paternal grandfather in the early 1840s. The acreage has been in my family ever since. I still occasionally hunt the same property my granddad did when he first came to Texas. I shot my first whitetail there, using a single-barreled 12 gauge that belonged to my maternal grandfather. My dad started hunting deer there and my daughters started hunting there as well! Traditions run strong in the South.

One of my first hunting trips with Bill Bynum took place in Tennessee. We hunted on his grandmother's place in western Tennessee near the Obine River, where Davy Crockett spent many days hunting deer and bear. Bill's family has owned the property since long before the Civil War. I hunted on the site of an old Civil War cemetery, along a creek where Davy Crockett, one of the Bynum ancestors, once trapped and hunted. I erected a ground blind at the base of the same tree where Bill shot several deer during his early years. It was special hunting on a traditional hunting ground.

Traditions often run deeper than simply hunting the same properties for several generations. Occasionally it becomes a tradition for all family members to shoot their first deer with the same rifle. Such is the tradition of the Mac Burns family, owners of the spacious Encinitos Ranch in deep South Texas. The rifle, a Winchester Model 92 chambered for the .44-40, once belonged to his wife's great-grandfather. All family members since have taken their first deer with that particular rifle. May that be a tradition of even longer standing.

Hunting whitetails is often a family tradition in the South, where daughters and sons hunt with fathers, wives with husbands, and friends hunt with other friends, old and new. One thing they all share is a love for the outdoors, hunting, and white-tailed deer.

Chapter 2: Part I

Opening Day Tactics: Archery

Bill Bynum

The rising sun cast its golden rays like an endless sea. Less than a hour had passed since I had taken my position. High in the portable tree stand, I could see across the vast soybean field. Like the three previous mornings, I stood silently watching the field. Hopefully this morning would be a replay of the past two mornings, and I would see numerous deer feeding near my stand.

If the deer followed their usual patterns, I would soon be drawing my bow. If not, I would have to figure out what had gone wrong. This is common practice when hunting the opening day, the day when the animals should not be influenced by hunting pressure, the day when everything is supposed to be right!

The opening day of a hunting season is always special to a dedicated hunter. This is the time for which we have all waited and prepared. Over the years I have learned that preparation is the key to successful hunting. Preparing for the first day of hunting requires the hunter to understand the various elements of hunting. One such element is animal behavior. Hunters having a working knowledge of a deer's behavioral patterns should be successful. Learning these patterns can be accomplished in different ways. One such manner is personal observation.

Observing deer in their natural habitat requires extensive time in the field. Of course, in most cases, hunters are not permitted this amount of time; therefore, they rely upon other forms of information to develop an opening day strategy. Their information is gleaned by talking to friends or by seeking advice as we are now doing. Therefore, I will relay some of my opening day strategies.

Learning The Habitat

Without question, one of the key elements in any hunting strategy is in finding the game. Without the presence of deer it is hard to have a successful deer hunt. This is why I spend as much time as possible in the field inves-

Bill Bynum believes preseason scouting can lead hunters to quick success.

The use of maps can lead hunters to prime hunting quickly and efficiently.

tigating. Many hunters term this time in the field as scouting, but I do not! I define all early field time as *learning the habitat.* The week before and all the time after opening day is scouting to me. I feel this way because I know the habitat will define most of the animal's movements. This is due to the three primary functions of a deer, functions I refer to as *eating, sleeping,* and *reproducing* the species.

During the early days of summer, I investigate the given habitat, or hunting area thoroughly. I try to learn where every food source, watering location, bedding area, etc., is located. When I discover key locations I record them on paper for future reference. These records will help in locating the animals during certain conditions.

Wise hunters know the existing conditions will dictate the animal's behavior. Experienced hunters also know that most existing conditions will change with the opening day of hunting season. This is due to human interference within the habitat (hunting pressure). We should also take note of any seasonal changes.

Most archery seasons begin in late summer and early autumn. During this time period, many changes can be found in the food sources. With these changes many of the deer's daily habits will change also. This is especially true when dealing with agricultural crops such as corn, soybeans, clover, etc. When these foods are available, they are excellent locations for hunting.

Hunting Entrance Points

Hunting agricultural crops requires the hunter to locate entrance points. Entrance points are areas where the deer enter the field to feed. These locations will usually be near some type of cover where the deer have been bedding. Locating entrance points can be achieved by scouting the edges of the field. Look for areas producing the highest amount of tracks. Upon locating these areas, try to discover the trail or trails the deer are following. It will be these trails that will play an important role in establishing an ambush site.

Establishing an ambush site on the edge of a field may be difficult. In some cases, there may not be enough cover to conceal the hunter, but if there is, this is an excellent location from which to hunt.

Hunting the edges of a field requires a hunter to be conscious of his or her surroundings at all times. Hunters must take precaution not to disturb the feeding area since walking through the preferred feeding area could cause alarm to the deer. Avoid entering the precise area when traveling to and from the hunting site. The more natural the area remains, the better!

In many cases, the actual food source will not support a proper ambush site. This is usually due to the open nature of the field; therefore, the hunter must intercept the deer traveling to or from the food source.

Once the trail has been established, it is time to locate the exact stand site. Before selecting the exact stand site, a few factors should be taken into consideration.

Which Trails?

One such factor is the type of trail that is being hunted. Basically, I place trails in two different categories. First there are the *secondary* trails. Secondary trails may be difficult to locate as they do not receive a lot of travel. In most cases, these trails will intersect at some point with the *primary* trail.

Primary trails are the major travel routes used by the majority of the deer. Primary trails will have the appearance of being worn or highly disturbed. Fresh dirt along primary trails relates directly to the amount of use the trail is receiving. The more activity the trail is receiving, the better the ambush site.

Another important factor in establishing the ambush site is the prevailing wind direction. Never position the stand so the air currents will travel towards the deer. Whenever possible, place the stand in a *downwind* position. If a downwind position is not possible, a *crosswind* location is second best.

Hunting agricultural food sources such as soybeans, corn, millet, etc., is usually limited as these food sources will be depleted or harvested within a given time period.

Learning *all* the preferred foods of the deer within a given habitat is important. Therefore, when one food source depletes, knowledge of another source is essential. The most common of the sources is acorns. Without question, the acorn nut rates high on the whitetail's grocery list. This nut is produced from oak trees. Among the whitetail's food sources the acorn is one of the most important.

Hunters who remain calm will reap the rewards of bow hunting.

In the southern United States there are numerous types of oak trees. Among the most common are the red oak, white oak, pin oak, scrub oak, black oak, and chestnut oak. Any given habitat may contain one or more species of oak trees. Knowing the preferred species of the acorn is important to the hunting strategy. Of the various types of oaks found, the white oak is the most preferred. The red oak and the pin oak will be the next in order. The reason for these choices is due to the tannic acid that is found in the acorns. The white oak acorn contains the least amount of acid, which results in a sweeter taste.

Locating the trees that have the preferred acorns can be done by tree identification. Positive identification can easily be made by the shape of the tree leaves and the tree bark. One of the methods I have come to rely on is the location of squirrel nests. These clusters of leaves inform me of the areas of the highest squirrel population. The value of this knowledge is that squirrels also feed on acorns. As a rule of thumb, the squirrels will have first choice before the deer. Many times these "nests" will be used for storing part of the winter food supply. In summary, if the squirrels like the area, the deer should also!

In some cases the opening day of archery season will be somewhat warm. Depending upon the region, the temperatures can even be downright hot! Therefore, weather conditions will play a role in our hunting. Personally, I believe the temperature will affect the hunter more than the deer. The reason being, nature has provided Mr. White-tailed Deer with excellent thermal protection. Under most southern temperatures a deer will remain comfortable whereas hunters may not.

Heat during the archery season can affect the hunter in many ways. The most common factor is in perspiration or sweating. The more we perspire, the more human scent we create. This, in turn, provides the deer with a better advantage in detecting the hunter's presence. This is the reason that I place a lot of emphasis on controlling my scent.

Staying Cool

Without question, one of the key factors in controlling human odor is to avoid getting sweaty, thus the reason I hunt in light-weight clothing. Over my clothing I wear a mesh-type camouflage suit that helps me to remain cool while walking to my hunting site.

Another special precaution I use in preparing my stand site is to cover my scent at the site. This preparation is done days before I ever hunt the area. To prepare my stand site, I take a clean cloth and tie it around the tree from which I will be hunting. I prefer to place the cloth approximately one foot from my hunting elevation. This will permit my covering agent to work, as I will describe in Chapter 9.

An additional foul-up performed on opening day is becoming over-excited. Remaining cool and calm at the sight of a deer walking into range is difficult. Perhaps it is this thrill that keeps us going back. But a few things that might help a little is practicing before the big day.

Practicing nerve control is done from a secondary stand site. Select a site that will not be hunted in the opening days of the season. From this site, spend a few days allowing deer to move around you. Imagine you are drawing your bow and other mechanics related to taking a shot. Remember that it is a combination of factors that will influence the outcome of the opening day.

Chapter 2: Part II

Opening Day Tactics: Gun

Larry L. Weishuhn

I clutched my Savage Model 340, chambered for the .30-30 Winchester, tightly when I heard a distant shot. It was opening morning and the woods were starting to come alive. Squirrels scampered about the forest floor picking up acorns and storing them for lean days of the coming winter. From my perch high in an old cedar tree I could see a couple of scrapes under a hickory tree and several rubs made on small cedar saplings.

Summer, when bucks are in velvet, is an excellent time to learn about the local deer herd.

Ron Porter, while on a wild hog hunt in late winter, checks an impressive rub, used for at least the past couple of years by various bucks.

Since the middle of the summer I had been scouting the area behind our camp for deer sign, looking for tracks, droppings, and places where deer browsed. As opening day approached, which seemed to come slower than Christmas, I spent every spare moment when not in school or taking care of chores, trying to learn about the local deer herd.

In our specific area of Colorado County, Texas, bucks started rubbing on trees and saplings in late August and making scrapes in late September, or at least by the middle of October. Most of the bucks in our hunting area were relatively young, and few ever lived long enough to mature. Even though they may have been young, these bucks made many rubs and scrapes.

Bowhunting was still in its infancy in Texas. Primarily I used the archery season to scout the areas I intended to hunt once the "real" deer hunting season started.

While hunting with a bow I spotted a good-sized buck, for our area, feeding on persimmons. He was too far for a shot, but I watched him eat his fill and then move on. Two days later I saw him in the same area. But again he stayed well beyond bow range. Thankfully both times that I saw him, he never knew I was in the area. When rifle season opened about two weeks later, I knew where I wanted to hunt. Shortly after daylight the first morning of rifle season the same buck I had seen during archery season seemed to simply appear in the tall bluestem grass near my stand in the tall cedar. A short time later I stood admiring my best buck up until that time. That was back in 1965. Had I simply been lucky, or had pre-

Maintain a "Buck Journal" to record the places where rubs, scrapes, and shed antlers are found, such as the one kept by Larry Weishuhn.

season scouting paved the way to my success? Actually it was likely a combination of both. However that experience taught me the value of scouting the areas I intend to hunt for whitetails.

Scouting Begins

Scouting for the next season should actually start as soon as the current season closes. Give the area a few days' rest, then go back and learn everything you can about the deer in the area. After the season closes, deer do not pay much attention to humans in their home area. The same amount of "disturbance" in a mature buck's territory during the fall might cause such a buck to change his patterns or habits, possibly even making him become totally nocturnal. Thus, winter is the best time to learn as much as you can about where bucks made rubs and scrapes. Both are still quite evident.

For years I have maintained extensive maps of the places I hunt year after year in my "Buck Journal." The journal provides me with a place to record other deer information. During my winter scouting trips I mark on maps where I find rubs and scrapes, as well as shed antlers. These are positive buck signs.

Cast antlers, especially those shed by bucks during the winter, provide the finder with considerable information about the buck that dropped them. They indicate where the buck was at a particular time. A shed antler also demonstrates that the buck survived the hunting season, tells you how large his antlers were during the hunting season just past and gives you some idea as to his age. In a previous book for Krause Publications, *Hunting Mature Bucks*, I explained how to determine the relative age of a buck by looking at his shed antler and comparing the size of the pedicel attachment area to the beam just above the burr. Essentially young bucks have small pedicel attachment areas and small beams. Medium aged bucks have sizable pedicel attachment areas and main beam circumferences. Bucks in their prime have large pedicel attachment areas and even larger main beam circumferences. Older, over-the-hill bucks have large pedicel attachment areas and smaller beam circumferences.

I realize it is difficult to find shed antlers in many areas of the South, primarily because of ground vegetation and because nearly every four-footed creature in the woods chews on them. However, in some areas it is difficult to find shed antlers because there are not many bucks and because most are young and do not produce large antlers. But as more and more hunters are becoming interested in mature deer and are getting involved in quality deer management, I suspect finding shed antlers is going to become easier in the future.

On numerous occasions I have taken a buck only a matter of a few yards from where I found his shed antlers. On a scouting trip during the spring turkey season, I found the shed of a large eight-point. That fall I shot the old buck less than a hundred yards from where I found the shed. This same sort of thing has happened several times. Many

In some areas shed antlers are hard to find because nearly every creature in the woods chews on them, including rabbits.

of the better bucks I have shot, as well as those harvested by hunting partners, have been taken under similar circumstances.

Scouting takes many forms. While I do most of my scouting during the winter to get an idea where deer live during the late part of the hunting season, I also do some summer scouting to determine where deer live during the early part of the hunting season.

During the late part of the summer, deer generally are in the same sort of routine as they are during the archery season. For this reason bowhunters have a definite advantage when it comes to scouting and reaping its rewards. Nonetheless, if bowhunters spend too much time scouting the area they intend to hunt, they, too, will alter the patterns of the late summer deer. This is often what has happened in some areas by the time rifle season follows archery season, where both bowhunters and rifle hunters hunt the same ground. For that reason I often do my scouting during the late winter and early spring because it generally gives me a true picture of what deer are doing during the late fall.

When scouting I spend considerable time visiting with people who work in or travel through the areas I intend to hunt. Rural mail carriers are an excellent source of information, as are timber cruisers, farm workers, and ranch hands. While I put stock in what some hunters say, I do not heed the words of everyone I talk to. Most of us are rather protective of our individual hunting areas and do not readily give such information freely.

Visiting with rural mail carriers, farm workers, and ranch hands is an excellent way to learn about the local deer herd.

Larry Weishuhn with a big Oklahoma whitetail, taken opening afternoon as it chased a smaller buck out of an alfalfa food plot.

Do Your Homework

Scouting also means learning as much as you can about the area you hunt and the animals that live there. Take the time to learn what the deer in your intended hunting area eat throughout the year and what the preferred browse species and mast are during the fall. Ask almost any Southern deer hunter what deer prefer to eat in the fall and they will be quick to tell you acorns–specifically, white oak acorns. But what if there are no white oak acorns, then what? Deer also like beechnuts, but what if there are no beechnuts? When they are available, deer will eat persimmons, the fruit of honey locust trees and a great variety of other fruits and mast crops. However, if you do not know how to identify the trees that produce these mast and fruits, how will you know where to hunt?

Most state wildlife departments or state land-grant colleges produce brochures and bulletins with information about what deer eat in the basic habitat types of various states. Such information may also be available from the local Soil Conservation Service offices. These same institutions also supply information that explains how to identify the plants and where you can expect to find them. Such information is invaluable. You can also obtain similar information by attending regional wildlife or deer management seminars presented by wildlife biologists.

As hunting season approaches, if you have done your winter and summer scouting properly, you will have an excellent idea where to hunt come opening day. However, as mentioned, if you are planning on hunting where there has been considerable bowhunting pressure, you may want to hunt where the bowhunters on your property have not been hunting. While young bucks do not seem as affected by increased human activity in their home territory, mature bucks are a whole new ball game!

Greenfield and food plots are ideal places to ambush bucks on opening day. Farmers have known for years that deer are attracted to various agricultural crops such as corn, soybeans, alfalfa, and many others. In recent years we have seen food plots used as part of management programs to increase a deer herd's nutrition and to entice deer out of the woods and into the open. These have become extremely popular throughout the South. In a later chapter I will discuss hunting these food plots as the deer season progresses. Opening day tactics should include hunting on the edge of greenfields where you can cover the entire field. In the morning it is a good idea to move back away from the edge of the field, as most deer leave food plots before daylight and head back to their bedding areas. However, in the afternoon it is generally more productive to hunt on the food plots proper as deer enter the fields late to forage.

One morning well before daylight while hunting in Oklahoma on the western edge of "the South," my guide, Brown Delozier, and I worked our way to the edge of an alfalfa food plot on the edge of a brushy river bottom. Brown works for Greg Simons' Wildlife Systems, Inc., based in San Angelo, Texas. From first light until about 10 that morning, the first day of the rifle season, we saw several does and small bucks, but spotted them in the brush and woods near the field and not on it proper. During the middle of the day we hunted by trying to rattle up bucks from the dense thickets and the river bottom. That afternoon we again hunted the alfalfa. About an hour before dark a young eight-point fed into the middle of the field. A few minutes later we noticed that he became extremely nervous and started watching something just beyond where we could see. After what seemed like an eternity a big mature nine-point buck appeared, eyes bugged, hair standing on end, and ears pinched tightly against his neck. The younger buck started to leave. After he did, the big buck started feeding on the lush alfalfa. He was the kind of buck I had driven many hours to hunt and take. It did not take me long to make up my mind.

Opening day is an ideal time to take your deer but it is certainly and thankfully not the only time to do so.

Chapter 3

Hunting the Fringes

Larry L. Weishuhn

The whitetail is often described as an animal of the "edge." He best makes his living where two different types of habitat meet. These two areas generally provide both food and cover. But do not discount him as one of the most adaptable big game animals in North America. He has learned how to survive on the edge of pine forests, in river and creek bottoms, farmland, mixed hardwoods and pines, coastal flats, and arid brush lands. His kind has also learned to survive on the edge of towns and big cities. One of the best bucks I ever saw in eastern Texas was within the city limits of Houston, and not that far from downtown. These days it is hard to find a place where his kind does not exist in the South.

This raises an interesting point. Most of us who hunt white-tailed deer tend to want to hunt where the brush and forest are the thickest, those spots as far from camp and civilization as possible. As a wildlife biologist/manager/hunter I have often seen some of the best bucks on the property close to camp. Perhaps this is simply another way they live on the edge.

On one of the ranches I managed for a while there lived an "interesting" buck. I had practically seen him grow up. The first time I saw him he was a rather small six-point. His main beams and tines were palmated. The buck started his life on property where hunters and landowner alike cared greatly for the resident wildlife. The hunters were involved in a quality management program where bucks were given the opportunity to mature to beyond four years in the presence of excellent year-round nutrition. The landowner grazed cattle, but did so responsibly, utilizing a rotational grazing system so the vegetation was never overgrazed. The hunting group also played their part by responsibly harvesting both bucks and does and planting food plots that provided forage for deer and other wildlife during the stress periods of late winter and late summer.

The Search Begins

Each year, for the first three years, when we conducted the annual deer census to determine the numbers of bucks and does the hunters would be allowed to take for the year, we saw the "palmate" buck. His

The white-tailed deer is an animal of the edge, normally where two habitat types come together.

antlers grew progressively larger each year. His spread widened, as did the width of the palmation on each main beam. By the buck's fifth fall he was a truly impressive buck. That year the hunters decided if they had an opportunity to take him, they would. That year the palmate buck disappeared. Prior to his fifth fall the buck was a regular at a food plot about a mile from the hunter's camp. The hunters tried hard to simply see the buck. But try as they may, he could not be found.

We failed to see the buck each of the next two years during our annual survey. I became concerned that the buck had died of natural causes or he had been killed and eaten by coyotes, or possibly a cougar that occasionally traveled through the property. However, I finally learned those assumptions were erroneous.

Between the county road leading to the property and the hunter's camp there was a small patch of woods and underbrush. Because it was close to the road and the house, and the woods were small, no one hunted it. That fall when we conducted our helicopter game survey I spotted a distinctive shed antler on the eastern edge of the small patch of woods. There was little doubt it had come from the palmate buck. Just as I mentioned seeing the cast antler to the pilot, I looked to my right and spotted the old buck with palmate antlers. Not only was the buck still alive, he had a great looking rack. It also became obvious the buck had moved to the small patch of woods where no one hunted, on the edge or fringes of the property between the county road and the hunter's camp. That same fall the wife of one of the hunters shot the buck on opening day, in the small patch of woods. I strongly suspect the buck moved to the woods near the front gate because it was on the fringes of where the hunters spent most of their time each fall.

Mature bucks that survive several years have a way of adapting to hunting pressure. The woods where the buck moved to truly provided a lot of "edge." It provided the necessities of cover and food at certain times of the year. The relatively open area around the woods also provided food during other times of the year, as well as allowing great visibility of any approaching danger. If danger approached, he simply disappeared into the small patch of woods. There he had plenty of hiding places.

The shed antler and my chance sighting of the buck definitely led to his undoing. The moment the buck saw the helicopter he disappeared into the small patch of trees and underbrush. He did not come out. The entire wooded area was only about two acres in size. After the survey we picked up the shed and found a couple of other antlers that had been cast by the buck.

The day before the opening of the season one of the hunters who had been involved in the management program since its inception took his wife into the woods and pointed out a tree where he thought she should hunt the next morning. Well before daylight the lady hunter eased quietly into woods and crawled up the tree they had decided on the day before. About 20 minutes after daylight the buck made his way along a trail only a few yards from her perch and she shot it. It later caused quite a stir around camp.

Mature bucks quickly learn how to adapt to hunting pressure. Seldom do they leave their home areas, they simply learn how to avoid hunters.

Hunting the fringes where pine plantations and hardwoods or overgrown fields come together is an ideal place to ambush a good buck or doe, especially in the afternoon. The open or grown-over fields provide food and the pine plantation provides primarily cover. In most pine plantations, once the trees grow to 15 to 20 feet tall they shade out underbrush and weeds. As a result these areas provide little, if any, food for deer. However, these areas produce cover where the deer can hide. As the trees grow taller, shading out the possibility of any other on-the-ground vegetation, these areas provide hiding places where the deer can see any approaching danger. If they do see or sense anything suspicious, they can quickly and easily escape.

Normally Southern deer feed in relatively open areas and fields late in the afternoon. Occasionally you can find deer in the open areas in the morning, but generally they start leaving such places well before daylight, especially the bigger, mature bucks. By hunting the fringe areas where field and forest meet, a hunter's chances of seeing deer are increased. This point has already been made and will likely be made again and again.

Still-Hunting Or Still Hunting?

Many areas of the South are not really conducive to still hunting because of thick cover, or because of the amount of dry leaves on the

Larry Bridgeman with a good buck he took on the fringes.

ground. But where there are "edges" the chances of taking a deer by this method are greatly enhanced.

When still hunting the edges, it is important to spend much more time looking than walking. Most still hunters walk and move much too quickly! It is far better to spend 10 times as much time looking as walking. If you do so, your chances of seeing a deer before it sees you are increased dramatically.

The tools required for still hunting in the South are a good binocular, knowledge of the area you plan to hunt, and doing so only where you will not run into other hunters. It also requires patience, soft clothing that does not make much noise, and paying particular attention to keeping the wind in your face and the sun at your back whenever possible. While I do not have the patience of Job, I have learned the importance of being patient and persistent. Thankfully I have had the opportunity to hunt several places where I could still hunt along the edges of a variety of habitat.

In southwestern Georgia I have had the opportunity to hunt on a large parcel of land that only receives hunting pressure on the weekends. During the week the property is normally deserted. Thankfully my schedule has allowed me to hunt there during the week. By the time I get to hunt, the season has normally been underway for several days.

During a recent trip to the property, my host gave me several options of ways to hunt, including dropping me off in an area where there were numerous fields planted in rye and clovers, small tracts of planted pines, as well as hardwood ridges and creek bottoms. The area had everything

Still-hunting requires a lot of patience, and much more watching than walking.

a deer could want, or for that matter what a Southern whitetail hunter could want for hunting ground.

Just before being dropped off in total darkness I made certain I had a map of the area, a compass, some flagging tape, a couple of sandwiches and apples, a small bottle of water, as well as a pair of dry socks, should they be needed. All these along with other essentials were tucked into my fleece day pack.

After being dropped off, I made my way to an area where I intended to spend the first minutes of shooting light. I had found the spot the afternoon before while sitting in a tripod on the edge of a large food plot. While glassing the area I noticed several deer were hanging up in a patch of woods on the north side of the field. The plot of woods was thick, as was the underbrush on the forest's floor. A small neck of big trees connected this area to the big woods. The afternoon before, I had moved a ladder stand to one of those trees where I would have a commanding view of the trails that led from the big woods to the small patch of woods and the big food plot.

By the time I still hunted my way to the ladder stand it was well past shooting light. I'd seen several does and fawns while hunting slowly toward the blind. Once there, no sooner had I crawled into the stand than I saw movement in the tall bluestem grass about a hundred yards away. All I could see of the deer was a tip of his light-colored antlers. I strained through the 10X by 42 Simmons binocular and could count what looked like nine total points. I also scanned ahead along the route I thought the deer would take. It looked as if there might be an opening about 10 yards in front of where the deer was; if so, I might be able to make a shot. Hurriedly, I replaced the binocular with my .309 JDJ Contender handgun. Resting the Contender solidly on the ladder stand's shooting bar, I got ready to take a quick shot, should the buck follow the route I expected him to. Moments later I squeezed the trigger and recovered from the recoil just in time to see the deer fall. The "edge" between a food supply and the deep woods had yielded a good buck once again. My hunt had ended almost before it had started.

A year later I was again hunting the same area. According to my host, the year had been a tough one. There had been few acorns produced and the deer were not in the hardwoods. He felt the deer were likely hanging on the edges of the woods and primarily feeding in the food plots after dark.

I again chose to hunt during the middle of the week when there were no other hunters in the woods. That would allow me to still hunt, working the areas where fields, woods, and brush met. After sitting for the first hour of daylight and watching a relatively open area where there were several scrapes in a small area, albeit unsuccessfully, I decided to move on.

At that point I left my perch in an old oak tree and started walking to an area where tall native grasses met several small mottes. I strongly suspected the deer were bedding in these areas. If I could spot bedded deer before they saw me, there might be an opportunity to take a good buck. I also hoped to do some rattling, but I knew it was a little late to expect

Larry Weishuhn with a decent southern whitetail taken in Georgia.

much response. For the most part the rut was long over and bucks were more concerned about eating and survival than either fighting or sex.

With a brisk wind in my face and the morning sun angling over my right shoulder I eased along, taking a step then stopping to look and glass for 30 to 40 seconds before taking another step and repeating the process. If I saw a buck, I knew I would probably have to shoot quickly if he jumped and ran, or be required to hurriedly take a shot at a bedded buck. For that reason I carried two long sticks that I intended to use for a crossed shooting sticks rest, if the occasion for a shot occurred at anything but a running deer. I have long learned I shoot much more accurately from a rest than I do offhand, even if the shot is at close range.

About a hundred yards into my hunt I stopped at a likely looking place where I could see a scrape and a rub at the edge of a thicket. After the sounds of nature returned I started rattling horns. I continued rattling off and on for about five minutes, then waited an additional 20 minutes to see if anything would respond. When nothing showed I continued on my way.

After each step I spent considerable time glassing the ground ahead, to the sides, and even behind. Quite often when hunting an "edge" or on the fringes, I have had deer allow me to walk right by them, even though they may have nearly been stepped on, then wait to run until after I had walked past them. Nearly 200 yards and almost an hour later I spotted a glint of sunlight on antler. Unfortunately all I could see were the tips of a rack. Try as I may I could not make out the deer's body, bedded in grass and underbrush. Although I was not sure, I felt the deer was watching me.

My host had told me of a big, massive antlered buck he had seen several times in the area I hunted. Was this the buck? If so he had all things in his favor. I hesitated trying to move to a better position. Ever so slowly I lowered the binocular and tried to position the shooting sticks where they would provide a solid rest. Given time I could perhaps be ready for a shot whenever the buck decided to make a move.

The buck, some 125 yards away, obviously was watching me. Just about the time I positioned the shooting sticks and started raising the rifle to my shoulder, he made his move. I watched the buck jump to his feet, tuck his tail between his legs and simply melt into the thicket. He was gone in a flash. All that was left was my memory of a disappearing massive, multi-tined buck.

Five Magic Seconds

What had I done wrong? Perhaps not too much, other than I should have been ready to shoot as soon as I spotted him. Big bucks seldom give a hunter more than five seconds to see them, evaluate them, estimate the distance and make a killing shot. That is not a lot of time! But, what you do and how you respond during those brief few seconds often determines whether or not you get a shot.

I have done considerable hunting in Texas where there is a great variety of habitat and a tremendous amount of "edge." One of my favorite ways of hunting deer in Texas is still-hunting along the edge of thickets and scattered brush areas. Much of Texas' brush lands are so thick, if you get into the heart of the brush you cannot see farther than a few feet in any direction. Taking a deer in those areas by still-hunting is nearly an impossibility. However, if you hunt the edges where different types of habitat meet, things are different. Much of Texas is comprised of fairly large parcels of land where there is only minimal hunting pressure. On places where I still-hunt there are either no other hunters on the property or I know exactly where they are hunting so I can totally avoid those places. Safety must always be the primary factor in determining how you hunt.

During one outing the South Texas wind blew out of the north and was filled with moisture, a light drizzle. The temperature was in the high 30s. For South Texas weather, it was miserable! But from a hunting standpoint it was a day I had long waited for. The only drawback was I wear glasses and such weather can cause a "seeing" problem.

The area I wanted to still-hunt was a combination of several edges or fringe areas going from a ridge to a dry creek bottom. On the ridge there was dense brush. The slopes had a scattering of brush. Closer to the bottom was a long narrow prickly pear cactus "flat" and farther down was a dense stand of chaparral and mesquite that marked the dry creek bottom. I knew the deer could be anywhere in this large area. While the country was ideal deer habitat, the timing of the hunt was even better because the rut was in full swing. It was a nearly perfect hunting situation.

The wind and the lay of the land were such that I could weave back and forth across the various fringes while keeping the wind in my face.

I walked ever so slowly into the wind, stopping occasionally to glass the areas ahead and on either side of me, as well as stopping to wipe the accumulated mist from my glasses. I walked up within only a few yards of several deer. But they all were does, fawns, and yearling bucks. I knew there were mature bucks in the area since I had found several big shed antlers the winter before. I did not want to settle for a young buck. The ranch hand who worked the property had also told me of several big bucks he had seen in the area. I continued "working" my way slowly across the pasture, weaving back and forth from the top of the low ridge to the mesquite tree-lined creek bottom. Through the mist and fog I saw movement coming my way. After wiping the water from my lenses, I knelt behind a low bush and peered at the apparition through my binocular. A doe appeared, almost mysteriously out of a mist. As she walked my way, she flicked her tail back and forth and occasionally stopped to look back. She was acting terribly nervous. On she came, coming closer and closer. When she was about 25 yards away, I dropped the binocular and raised my Remington Model 700 chambered for the .280 Remington. I remained statue-like still and the doe walked right past me, totally unaware of my presence. Just then I saw the buck following her trail, his head low to the ground in typical rutting buck fashion. Actually he was the first of four bucks that were trailing the doe.

**Wading small creeks during the later part of the hunting season
can allow you to get close to bucks.**

The first buck was a big eight-point with massive antlers and about an 18-inch outside spread. Right behind him came another eight-point of nearly the same proportions. Next came about a 20-inch 10-point, but with relatively short tines. Right on his tail was a bigger buck with what looked like 12 typical points. Throughout my hunting career I have longed to take a typical 12-point buck. Finally it seemed here was to be my chance at such a buck.

I watched intently as the buck cleared some brush obscuring his shoulder. The moment he did, I squeezed the trigger. He went down in a heap. Anxiously I chambered another round, just in case it was needed. Thankfully it was unnecessary. Moments later I walked to where the buck lay and started counting his points. There were 6 typical points on his left side and 7 typical points on the right antler. I could hardly believe it. My first Typical greater than 12-point buck in nearly 40 years of hunting! He had an 18-inch outside spread with fair mass and relatively long tines. I was ecstatic! Hunting the fringes of several habitat types had paid off once again.

Hunting in the Old South is considerably different than hunting in the southwest portion of the South. In the South creeks generally have water in them. In the Southwest creeks are most often dry! Thus, hunting creek bottoms in the Southwest is nothing like hunting creek bottoms in the South. But regardless of where they are, small creeks seem to be gathering places for wildlife. Unfortunately these areas of the South are also home for the wiggly-snake kind of wildlife. If you are going to hunt the South's fringes, swamps, uplands or wherever, snakes are something you always have to be cognizant of. That does not mean you should fear them, but only be aware of their presence. They do represent potential danger–life threatening danger!

Creeks And Fringes

One of my favorite ways to hunt the fringe areas of the South country is to wade small creeks. But I personally do this only after the weather turns cold and snakes have long since slithered into their dens. If you move slowly when wading in a creek, the sound of your approach is covered by the gurgling of the flowing water. Many times while wading up or down a creek, I have been able to walk right up to deer.

Using the water to hide your sounds or approach is nothing new. Early hunters used this technique for many, many years. But I personally came upon this technique while I was a youngster. Squirrel hunting was a big deal back then, as it should be even today. To take my limit of squirrels I often waded up or down small creeks. One day while returning home from a successful squirrel hunt, I walked right up on the biggest buck I had ever seen in the area. He was feeding just off the edge of the narrow little bottom. He paid me no mind whatsoever. I have to admit for a moment I considered taking a shot at the deer with my single-shot .22 rimfire rifle. I knew I could kill the deer at that range and back then .22 rimfires were legal. I was hunting on my granddad's property and it was not that far from home. However, there was one little problem...it was not quite deer season. The season would not open for about another three weeks. After several anxious moments, combined with some really serious soul-searching, I walked away and left the big buck standing right there. Alas, I never did see the deer again.

That chance meeting left an impression on me. Since then I have walked up on deer several times while wading in the creek. That technique helped my friend and hunting partner of well over 20 years, Ron Porter, a retired New Mexico Department of Game and Fish game warden and administrator, take an extremely nice buck.

On one of the ranches I managed there lived an old buck. In the antler department he was not the greatest, but what he lacked in antlers he made up in hunter "savvy." Try as we may, we could not take this buck. Finally out of frustration as much as anything, Porter and I decided the best thing would be to have him walk in the middle of a little stream that traversed the property. I would walk the high ground in case he spooked the deer from the bottom.

Less than five minutes after we started walking I heard a shot. A few minutes later I joined Porter to admire the old buck and listen to his tale. Right after Ron started wading upstream he spotted a buck laying down next to a downed tree. The buck lay facing away from the water's edge. Ron slowly waded to the shore, his sounds covered by water flowing over rocks, and took careful aim with his customized .35 Whelen. To quote Porter, "I love it when a plan comes together."

Chapter 4

Pressured Bucks

Bill Bynum

The opening day of hunting season marks the day we have all been waiting for. This is the day we venture to the field to shoot the buck of our dreams. Sometimes the dream comes true; many times it does not. While we wait in our hunting stands we count the shots being fired around us. We know with each shot our chances become smaller. We also know the clock is ticking and the deer are being wiser. This is the way many hunters feel within the opening hours of hunting season.

Most hunters know the more hunting pressure an area receives, the tougher the hunting becomes. Many areas located east of the Mississippi River become nightmares for serious deer hunters; the reason being simply that the eastern portion of the United States contains the highest percentage of hunters. A vast number of these hunters are found in the southern states where deer seasons extend for months. This extension results in extreme high pressure upon the deer. This is due to extensive amounts of human involvement within the deer's habitat. It is this involvement we term as pressured hunting.

What Creates Pressured Hunting

Pressured hunting can be created in a number of ways. Basically pressured hunting is created by hunters. Not just inexperienced hunters, but 99.9 percent of *all* hunters!

Today there are few hunters who cannot go afield without leaving some form of human mark where they have been. In a nutshell, many skills of woodsmanship have been forgotten during the past few generations. Perhaps this is not as much the hunter's fault as it once was. Today our fast-paced society has diverted us from many of the pleasures our forefathers knew, pleasures such as not fighting a time clock or worrying if the truck is going to start!

Another key factor is that past generations had more hunting areas than we have today.

Experienced hunters know the importance of keeping the hunting area as natural as possible. Sadly, this is not always the priority of inexperienced hunters. These hunters do not often realize the mistakes they make that, in turn, educate the deer. Mistakes such as slamming car doors, yelling to each other, and disturbing the woods are just some of the common errors that educate deer to hunting pressure. What can be done to correct this problem?

Personally, I feel little can be done. The problem has existed for as long as I can remember. Unless one is fortunate enough to have hundreds of acres to hunt on alone, it's tough! In reality it is difficult to enter a deer's home ground without being detected. So if there is a solution, what is it? Don't ask me! I've been trying to think of one for years.

I have learned to place more emphasis on trying to outsmart the hunters instead of the deer! In doing so, I have dedicated over thirty years of my life. These have been years filled with many frustrations and pleasures. The frustrations would provide ample material for volumes of books. The pleasures are about to be given in this chapter.

Modern Technology Does Help

Modern technology within the hunting world has come a long way in recent decades. Today we can travel to the backside of a wilderness in our 4X4 pickup trucks, unload our ATVs, and go even deeper into the wilds! Once we arrive at our destination, out comes the super-duper bionic ear. We can even look into the next zip code with our rifle scope as we sit in the climb-a-vater tree stand.

Perhaps I am making a little fun of some of the gadgetry of modern day deer hunting, but fact is fact. What many hunters are forgetting is, no matter what we have, we are still in the whitetail's world; a world where the animal spends 365 days a year, a world where he is as familiar as we are with our homes!

Like all living creatures a deer's main priority is to survive. Luckily, the animals do not have guns so their natural reaction to an intrusion is to run. Once the animals have learned the warning signals of danger, they learn to *avoid* the danger. Hunters who learn to avoid alerting the deer become woods-wise in my opinion. Learning to become what I define as woods-wise is not difficult. It simply means thinking before we do something.

Take a few seconds to think what a deer will think the next time you cough in the woods or the next time you feel a little tired and drive the ATV to your stand site.

Naturally not all hunters make the same level of mistakes as others. Many hunters try hard to avoid some of the more common errors. It is these hunters who must learn to cope with hunting pressured deer. It is through these mistakes that I have learned to allow hunters to aid me in harvesting my deer.

Modern advancements make hunting more fun. But Bill Bynum believes in using them properly.

Bynum's First Law Of Hunting Pressured Deer

Finally, after years of hunting pressured deer I can say that it is not an impossible task. This is true if you believe in my first law of the subject. The law I refer to is "No Living Creature Is Perfect!" The definition of this is hunters must learn to capitalize upon the mistakes of both the deer and the hunters.

If the hunter practices good woodsmanship, the odds for success increase dramatically. By practicing good woodsmanship, we begin my second law of hunting pressured deer.

Bynum's Second Law

It is my opinion that few sportsman afield follow this suggestion. To me, it is a personal law: "Always Think Like A Hunter." This is a common mistake I feel all hunters commit at some time. Many deer hunting enthusiasts go afield with rabbit's feet and four-leaf clovers in every pocket. These sportsmen rely on the phenomenon of *luck* to harvest deer. A true hunter will understand his knowledge of the animal's

Big bucks such as this one requires looking in the right places.

habits and the habitat will make his "luck." This is the reason I place great emphasis on knowing the hunting habitat.

One of the first things I learned about hunting white-tailed deer was this: You can't shoot it if it isn't there! Knowing where the animal lives and what controls its movements are the keys to eating venison. This is why I feel that one of the most important elements of locating deer is proper scouting.

Scouting For Southern Bucks

If I have learned anything about deer hunting, it is that you simply must find them to shoot them! Sometimes locating a mature buck can be as difficult as finding a needle in a haystack. This is especially true if you are hunting a new area. It can also be a nightmare when hunting time is limited. These are a couple of the reasons I try to spend as much time as I can in the field. Learning all the factors that control a deer's habitat is not an easy task. But once the controlling factors are discovered, the fun can begin.

Many factors will influence where deer will be found during certain time periods. Learning how certain factors affect deer is one of the keys to finding them. Knowing the preferred areas of the animals during specific time periods will increase the odds for successful hunting. In deer hunter's vocabulary, the method for accomplishing this is called "scouting."

Scouting is one of the most critical elements responsible for providing a steady supply of venison. In most cases the hunter who formulates a strategy before going afield will unlock many of the mysteries of successful scouting.

Experience has taught me there are various forms or methods for scouting an area. All the methods are controlled by the hunter's knowledge of the area and the existing time frame. The time frame I refer to is one of the seasonal changes (spring, summer, autumn, and winter) that will be upon us. Each seasonal change brings forth a different set of conditions to the area or habitat. In short, the existing conditions upon the habitat will affect the animals' habits.

Experienced hunters will record these seasonal periods and the degree to which they change the daily functions of the deer. Knowing this degree of change in the animals' basic functions will become a key factor in successful hunting.

The basic functions of a deer are eating, sleeping, and reproducing the species. Therefore it is important to link the proper area to the specific function of the animal. Many times an area will contain all the elements needed (food, water, and cover) and many times it will not. Learning to interpret the contents of a specific area is the primary factor in proper scouting. This is not difficult for a skilled hunter who understands the elements pertaining to the surroundings.

The skills I refer to are the knowledge the hunter has obtained in learning the area, deer behavior, and woodsmanship. Before an area can properly be scouted the hunter must know the geographical ter-

The use of topographical maps are a must for finding trophy bucks.

rain of the hunting area. Knowing the geographical variations (terrain breaks) will aid in locating travelways used by deer. Deer, like fish, will use terrain breaks for movement.

Deer Are Smarter Than You Think

The variations in elevation will be based upon the advantages for seeing and smelling. I believe the elevation will depend on two factors. The first factor is if the deer wishes to overlook the surrounding area. During this mode we will find the animal in areas of higher elevation. An excellent example of this would be ridge tops overlooking fields

The second is if the animal wishes not to be seen. This mode will find the deer in lower elevated areas. Locations such as dry creek beds, drainage ditches, etc., can become quick travelways. These locations will vary with the amount of pressure within the given area.

The selected travelway will be influenced by the existing air currents and the elevation of the travelway. The reason for the air currents being such a factor is detecting scent.

Seasoned hunters know that 99 percent of the time deer travel facing into the air currents to intercept scent. Knowing the predominant wind direction of the area is important for stand placement. With this

Bucks such as this one are not dumb. It takes a wise hunter to discover where they live.

knowledge the preferred travel routes can be established before the hunt.

The need to travel to and from the strategic areas of food, water, and cover will always remain. These three vital factors influence deer survival and should become the foundation for forming a scouting strategy. Knowing where food sources, water, and cover are located within the area is critical to hunting success. Learning the travelways to and from these areas will be the key to forming the hunting strategy.

The existing time period is an important factor when forming a scouting strategy. This is especially true in the southern states were food, water, and cover are usually abundant. This abundance can inspire numerous behavior patterns among the deer. One day the deer can be feeding upon one food source and something else the next day. This is the reason hunters must know what food sources are being used and when. What does this have to do with hunting pressured deer? Simple. The animals must maintain the elements of survival at all times. This is one of the key elements in hunting pressured deer. You should be prepared to take advantage of the opportunity when the deer presents it. In short, learn to ambush the deer.

Learning To Ambush

In my opinion the more a hunter learns the art of ambushing, the more successful the hunter will be. Learning to be at the right place at the right time is the answer. This is accomplished by having a working knowledge of the animals' behavior patterns and the habitat. This is why I try to learn every square inch of the given habitat; learn where each of the animal's preferred food sources is located; learn where the terrain supports ideal bedding cover; learn where all the trails that link the animals' needs are located. Once these three key factors are discovered, a hunting strategy can begin.

This is also the reason I begin planning my hunt a year in advance. That's right, one year in advance! It is my belief that once a deer living in a pressured area survives one hunting season, it learns where the safety zones are located. This means the animals learn which trails afford the safest travel, etc. I define these trails as *pressure trails*. Learning these preferred locations can be accomplished during the days immediately following the close of hunting season. During this time frame the animals will still be under the influence of the hunting pressure. If the area affords good tracking media (snow, sand, or mud), the prime trails can be easily identified. If there is difficulty in establishing the trails, another course of action can be used.

Tricks Of The Trade

In years past I have learned that the old saying, "Where there is a will, there is a way" is true. Establishing primary pressure routes can be accomplished even if there is no tracking media available. The way I do this is simple and requires only some legwork and a spool of sewing thread. I tie strands of thread across every trail I have located. The strands of thread are placed in six-inch intervals beginning two feet from the ground and extending up to five feet. If the upper strands of thread become broken, I can safely assume the antlers of a buck did the deed.

Next I clear large areas of debris from the trails with my foot. This will give me a general idea of the number of animals passing through the area. The next phase is to wait 24 hours before checking each of the trails. All my findings are then recorded on my map. This will be the valuable information that will lead me into the upcoming hunting season.

The Record Book Theory

Like most hunters, I have read a lot about the many ways of collecting educated deer. Some of these words of wisdom have helped me during a few hunts, I think! Some of the so-called teachings merely confirmed that a few authors should be spending more time in the field away from their computer keyboards.

Hunting an animal as intelligent as a three-plus-year-old buck is tough. A white-tailed buck that has survived numerous hunting seasons is a smart animal. This is the reason I base my trophy status on the animal's age instead of its antler size. Most bucks perish before they reach 19 months of age in the eastern United States. Therefore, I am a firm believer that, in order to harvest a buck three years old or

Bill Bynum displays a mature buck. He feels the age status is an element of trophy status.

older, a hunter must be dedicated to the cause. This means that countless hours will be spent locating the buck. Then many hours will pass waiting for the animal to make a mistake. This all adds up to a lot of time spent in the field–time few hunters are privileged to have to spend chasing a record class buck. In reality, few hunters ever get to see a trophy buck aged three years old or older. To constantly harvest animals of this classification is even harder. This is the reason I place more value on the *cookbook* then the *record book*.

Deer hunting is a sport that should be measured in terms of personal satisfaction. Deer hunting is a privilege that we should all enjoy and value. Hunting is a reward and no animal should be discriminated against by any means. I feel that every white-tailed deer is a trophy! Only a true hunter knows what is his/her trophy. In short, a trophy is judged in the eyes of the beholder.

Chapter 5

Greenfield Strategies

Larry L. Weishuhn

The farmer stopped his tractor and walked over to where I waited at the gate leading into his field. We exchanged pleasantries as he wiped his forehead with a red bandanna. After visiting about the weather, the current price of corn and fat cattle and how his family was, we got down to the real reason for my being there. Some time ago the farmer and I had started talking about the white-tailed deer that resided on his property. Initially the old farmer had seen them simply as competitors for his crops, but after several visits he was starting to see deer in another light.

His property was of great interest to me. Not only did the farmer own the property he farmed, he also owned a large tract of timberland next to the farmed land. Based on deer sign seen on the property when I had first gained permission to hunt squirrels on his acreage, I knew it could provide some excellent deer hunting and big bucks.

It took several visits before he would talk to me about deer, other than fussing about them. I doubted seriously he knew I was a biologist for the state wildlife department or that I had intentions of eventually leasing the deer hunting rights on his property. Several landowners in the area had only recently started leasing hunting rights and if I had my way, this farmer would soon be leasing to me.

While we talked he mentioned baling hay and that the boys who usually helped him haul it had left for college. I saw the ideal opening and volunteered to help. That afternoon he and I hauled a couple hundred bales of hay and really got to know each other.

The timing seemed perfect to ask him about leasing his property. When I did, he replied he would be glad to lease the hunting rights on his property to me. Over the next few weeks we worked out several details, including the fact that I would be able to add four or five other hunters, of my choice and approved by him, to help finance our agreement.

When we got the group together, one of the first things we did was to work a deal with the landowner to plant food plots and pay him to leave several rows of corn in the field along the edge of the fence lines and along the edge of the woods. With that we were almost ready for the hunting season.

Every opportunity that we had, we spent scouting the new property. We also devoted considerable time visiting with the owner to find out where he had seen deer, particularly bucks. Essentially all deer looked the same to him and anything with "horns" was a big buck. Even so, his information proved extremely valuable.

Select The Right Opening Day Stand

With the hunting season fast approaching, I set up a stand in a tall oak overlooking a cornfield on one side and a wheat patch on the other side.

Larry Weishuhn with a buck taken early in the season as it fed into a food plot.

Hunting directly on food plots during the first few days of the hunting season can produce excellent results. A shooting house such as this hides your movement.

I felt assured of being able to shoot a deer there on opening day. The first morning of the hunt I headed to an area with several oaks. It had not been a good acorn year but I had found a couple of trees that had produced a fair mast crop. The morning passed without any great happening, other than seeing several does, fawns, and five young bucks, all six and eight points, but none that tempted me. My intentions were to shoot a mature buck and eventually take a couple of does to help lower the overall population. The bag limit in the area was a total of four deer but no more than two could be bucks.

That afternoon I crawled into the big oak at about two o'clock. The first deer to come to the field were does and fawns. At four o'clock the first buck appeared, a young eight point. About 10 minutes later I spotted a much bigger buck. All I could see were his head, antlers, and a small portion of his neck. He appeared to be a good one for the area. He was tall and had 10 long points.

The buck watched the does in the field and was totally unaware of my presence. Satisfied there was no apparent danger, he strode into the field. A hasty look told me the buck was big-bodied and definitely mature. I could also see he had a fair amount of loose skin about his face and was a bit pot-bellied. The old 7X57 with its variable scope came up easily. When the crosshairs settled on the deer's shoulder, I squeezed the trigger. The deer simply fell to the ground. All that I could see of him was one of his main beams sticking out above the tall wheat. That night there was a celebration around the campfire. The big 10 point had a 20-inch spread on long beams, supporting tines between four and nine inches in length.

The following afternoon a fellow lease holder hunted my food plot stand. Just before dark he, too, was able to take a good 10 point buck that was nearly a mirror image of my opening day, greenfield buck. Thereafter we only occasionally saw mature bucks on that food plot, but there was no shortage of does and young bucks that fed there every afternoon.

During the early season it is a good idea to hunt right on the field where you have a commanding view of it. Bucks and does are less wary about coming into fields the first few days of the season. Thereafter, the bucks become a bit more wary. Early in the season deer tend to forage in food plots more in the afternoon than in the morning. However, do not think this is a set-in-stone rule. Occasionally, big bucks feed in food plots in the morning.

While on a hunt in Georgia with Realtree Camo's Bill Jordan, we were joined by Woody Aytes of Missouri. Mister Woody, a retired Missouri Highway Patrolman, was on his first true Southern whitetail hunt. The area we hunted was primarily cut-over timber land interspersed with hardwood ridges and creek bottoms, which provided not only tremendous cover but an ideal food supply. Also scattered throughout the property were several small food plots planted specifically for whitetails. The area oak trees that year did not produce a good mast crop. What few acorns there were quickly disappeared. Based on the sign we saw, the deer had shifted primarily to the food plots as their source for food. Not only that, we found numerous scrapes right along the edge of a couple of the plots. It was at one of these greenfields that Mister Woody decided to take a stand.

Even though the season had been open for a while, our area had only been lightly hunted and it appeared (determined by brushing out trails) that most of the deer were feeding in the fields sometime during the morning.

The first morning on his food plot Mister Woody only saw a couple of does. That afternoon he saw several more does but only one small buck. The following morning he was back at the same food plot. Only a few minutes after eight he heard a noise behind him in the brush. Turning to face that direction, he saw a buck walking along at a pace like an animal going somewhere in particular. Before he could react, the buck was gone. Minutes later the buck reappeared at the food plot's edge, freshened a scrape, and then began feeding in the field. When he turned broadside it took Mister Woody only one shot from his favorite .30-06 to claim his first southern deer. Hunting a food plot had paid a handsome dividend.

In a similar situation a couple of weeks later, I hunted property several miles west of Georgia. This land had a couple of pivot irrigation systems where alfalfa and other hay crops were planted. The side benefit was the pivots produced an ideal food source for the area's white-tailed deer.

I had seen some good bucks in the area on a previous hunt a couple of years earlier. On that occasion the bucks were seen in a series of brushy

Woody Aytes with a good Georgia buck he took as it fed into a greenfield.

creek bottoms that bordered the hay fields. I suspected the creek bottoms were where I would end up hunting. Little did I know my hunt would be over nearly before it began.

Pay Attention To Those Who Live On The Property You Hunt

The night before the hunt the property owner suggested I accompany him in the morning for a swing through his property. He would pick me up at the bunkhouse at just about daylight and we would make "a round." I have long ago learned it is a good idea to do nearly whatever your host asks of you.

I got up well before daylight and made coffee. The sky in the east was already pink and rosy when my host arrived. He drove up, walked in, and took off his coat. We began visiting about his ranch and where he hoped to go with his wildlife program. I was interested in his program but at the moment I was much more interested in looking for a big whitetail. The sun was just about to peak over the horizon when he finally suggested we go see if we could find a whitetail. We started to back out of the driveway. Suddenly he stopped and started pulling back up to the bunkhouse. For a moment I thought he might have forgotten something.

'I think you ought to go check the field just below the bunkhouse before we leave. There's been a big eight point seen just below the house several different times. I'd hate to leave without checking the field,' spoke the manager. I seriously wondered whether a big whitetail would be so close to the bunkhouse, the road, and two neighbors' houses complete with several "yard" dogs. Reluctantly I walked to the yard fence just below the bunkhouse and peered across the wide open field. There some 600 yards away was a buck, a big eight point with massive beams spread way beyond his ears. There was little doubt the buck piqued my interest. The hard part, though, was trying to get close enough for a shot.

My host suggested that I allow him to drive me to the edge of the small creek bottom that paralleled the field. A couple of minutes later he dropped me off and I started my stalk. My biggest concern was there might be other deer in the creek bottom that would spook the deer out of the field before I could get within range. Before I really started the stalk, I ran into my first doe. Thankfully she never saw me and started feeding into the thicket along the creek bottom. About 200 yards farther on I came upon a small buck working a scrape. I waited until he moved into the deeper part of the creek bottom. All the while, however, I was getting anxious about what might be going on with "my" buck, last seen feeding on the lower end of the pivot system.

Ever so carefully I eased toward the edge of the cover, almost expecting the big buck to have moved off into the creek bottom at the end of the field. Much to my surprise the buck was not only still there but he had moved to within about 350 yards and into the center part of the field. He had bedded down in the wide open. There would be no way to get closer! I set up my crossed shooting stick, got comfortable on the rest, cranked the scope power ring up to 10, took several breaths to set-

Larry Weishuhn with a 22-inch wide 8 point taken at long range as it fed in a food plot early in the hunting season.

tle down, and started squeezing the trigger. At the shot from my custom MacGillivray .280 Remington, the buck simply slumped in his bed and was dead. Less than 30 minutes after legal shooting time, I had a massive, long-tined eight point buck on the ground, taken at long range in a greenfield.

Hunting food plots is not always quite as easy as taking the two bucks described. Quite often it involves considerably more sitting and watching and sometimes not really hunting on the food plot itself but along trails leading to it.

Once the deer season has been open for several days and there has been a fair amount of hunting pressure in and around the food plots, it is a good idea to do some scouting to determine what trails the deer are taking into the fields. Once you determine the trails used, follow them into the woods for a distance. If you can see tracks, look for areas where it appears that several trails converge. Such a place is an excellent area to set up a tree stand.

Mature Bucks Are Different

Mature bucks seldom enter greenfields until after dark. However, that does not mean they do not come close to entering them. Instead they will "set up" where several trails come together and "check" every doe that comes by, this shortly before, during, and even after the rut. If they

Trails leading to food plots are ideal places to set up on to watch for a mature buck. He may spend time here checking out the does that head to the field.

find a receptive doe, the merry chase is on. If they do not find a receptive doe, they will stay in the immediate area until after dark, before venturing into the field.

The distance from the edge of a greenfield to where you should set up to hunt a big mature buck depends on the woods and brush that surround it, as well as the behavior of the local deer. It also makes a considerable difference how far deer travel from their bedding areas to the

Larry Weishuhn with the buck he took at a "staging area" leading to a food plot.

Chances at taking big mature bucks are increased by hunting away from the edge of a food plot, where they generally wait for darkness to arrive before heading into the greenfields.

greenfield. In most instances, however, you generally want to set up 50 to 100 yards from the edge of the field. This is where the bucks will generally set up something similar to a staging area. If the area you hunt has soil that is conducive to reading tracks, you can especially get a good idea of where to set up. Look for areas where, as mentioned earlier, several trails come together. Then look for a set of tracks that seem to pace back and forth across these trails. Generally such a track was made by a buck. Set up your tree stand in the general area, using the wind and sun to your advantage. You do not want to set up directly in these staging areas, but close enough where you can watch these spots. If you get too close you are likely to spook not only the buck but the does using those trails as well.

One fall the deer on a ranch I was managing were really feeding in our food plots. The only problem was the mature bucks were feeding in the fields only after dark. That being the case, we set up a couple of blinds on one of the buck staging areas, actually about 30 yards from where it appeared that a buck had walked back and forth across three different trails where they converged. He had also made a scrape alongside one of the trails. By the size of the scrape and the footprint he left in it, the buck was a good one!

About midafternoon I still-hunted my way into where I had hung a stand. I knew it would be a while before deer started making their way to the bean field, but I wanted to be there well ahead of time to keep from spooking any deer that might be in or traveling through the immediate area. It was nearly an hour after I climbed into my stand before the first deer appeared, a doe with her nearly grown fawn. They never slowed down as they headed to the field. Only a few minutes later the first buck appeared, a young, two-year-old eight point. He moved slowly and cautiously toward the scrape. After freshening the scrape, the buck backed up next to the most frequently traveled of the three trails. He waited there patiently for the first doe to come along; his wait was not long. A large doe came at a fast walk. As she walked past the buck, he made a move on her. Initially she turned to face him, then almost immediately took off at a fast walk. The buck lowered his head in typical rutting behavior and followed her. The two disappeared into the brush.

Ten minutes later a much bigger buck started walking toward me. I nearly shot him, but then decided to wait to see what he would do. He, too, visited the scrape, scraped the ground three times with his left and right foot, chewed on the overhanging limb, and urinated in the scrape while dribbling urine down his hocks and into the scraped area. His scraping activity taken care of, he walked to the edge of the trail close to where the younger buck had waited. He stood there watching the trails, waiting for a doe to walk past. I strongly suspect he would have picked up the trail of the first receptive doe that came past. I did not give him a chance. When the five-year-old 19 inch, 10 point presented a clear shot, I squeezed the trigger on my .309 JDJ Contender handgun.

As the hunting season progresses and the rut starts waning, food plots again are important. During the rut the bucks visit the greenfields not only for food, but also because of the social aspects of finding receptive does. After most or all of the does are bred, bucks once again become interested in eating and trying to repair their bodies after the rigors of the breeding season. During this time you may be able to find deer in food plots at any hour of the day. It is also not uncommon to find big bucks bedding down in food plots, especially in standing corn, bean, or any other of the taller food plot plants. Never overlook hunting taller standing food plots.

Hunting food plots can be fun, challenging, difficult, and also rewarding. Food plots also play an important role in the managing of southern whitetails.

Chapter 6

Hunting Clear-cuts

Bill Bynum

Like most of my hunting colleagues, much of my hunting knowledge has come from personal experience–experience gained in the field while pursuing the mighty white-tailed deer. Much of this experience was gained through trial and error, which consists of trying some idea until I was sure it simply would not work, then trying it again just to be sure!

Today I can proudly say, "I still have a lot to learn about hunting the magnificent white-tailed deer." The words of my beloved friend James, alias "Pap" Holt, still ring in my memory. "By the time you learn it all, if you ever do, you are too old to use it!" I really feel ol' Pap just may have something there, but there are some lessons I have learned.

The greatest of the lessons is that one must think like a hunter to become a hunter. People who drive to a strange area, sit on the hood of their car, and shoot a deer are not hunters in my opinion. These people are simply sportsmen on a holiday who got lucky!

True hunters, in my opinion, love the very thought of matching wits with the game they are pursuing–it's that simple! Hunters thrive on the challenge of hunting a deer within its given habitat, enduring all the elements involved with becoming both a sportsman and a hunter.

One form of southern deer hunting that will test a hunter's skills is hunting the clear-cuts. Clear-cuts are areas in which most or all of the timber has been harvested. Upon harvesting the area, it is then replanted with seedling trees. This is a common practice of most timber companies. In many ways this is much better than some other forms of land practices I have seen–hats off to the companies that care about us!

Hunting The Clear-cuts

Not all clear-cuts are created equal. Hunters selecting a clear-cut should first analyze it. When analyzing a clear-cut, the first factor involved is the age of cutover. The reason for this is the clear-cut may not have anything to offer the deer. Hunters must remember an area must provide either food or cover for the deer.

True hunters love the thrill of matching wits with a buck, as this hunter has done.

Sawing Into The First Stage

Before a clear-cut can become a clear-cut, the mature timber must be cut down. In many cases the remains of the harvested timber (tree tops) will be on the ground. These remains can provide both food and cover for the deer. Many hunters are led to believe the sound of chainsaws frighten deer. On the contrary! I have witnessed deer travel to the sound of chainsaws. The deer know the sound of a chainsaw means easy pickings. And if this means easy pickings for the deer, what about the deer hunter! In most cases hunters will discover a deer hunting paradise during this stage.

Burned And Bare

Some timber companies do not allow the remains of cutting to last. Often the fresh-cut areas are burned and replanting is done quickly. Though this sounds like a bad dream for the deer, it isn't. From this burning, minerals are placed into the ground and nature will begin her course of action. It will get better, wait and see!

Prime Time Clear-cuts

Clear-cuts that have been burned can become hunting paradises for those who wait. Within a two-year span from the time of burning, new life begins. With the restoration of the ground, plant life flourishes. The countless seedling trees that were planted have grown rapidly. With this restoration in life, both food and cover have been provided for the deer. In short, hunters, by passing clear-cuts ranging two to five years in development, don't know what they are missing.

Father Time Dominates

Like everything else in life, trees grow old, too. Because of this, clear-cuts become mature forests. In most cases the clear-cuts of yesterday become the pine forests of today. But within these pine thickets, nature usually provides various hardwood trees: red oak, white oak, and other nut-bearing trees are common among southern pine forests. It is along the bottom of these trees that hunters will discover their bounty, but for the thinking hunters these areas will become only one of their many haunts.

If there is one thing that really tickles me, it's watching the expression on my buddies' faces when I nail a nice buck. The sight of the buck makes them look as if they've just encountered a UFO. This is especially true when the hunting conditions are poor!

This occurred a few years ago when some friends and I hunted some clear-cuts. We'd learned the clear-cuts were approximately six to eight years of age. We had heard rumors of some trophy bucks in the area and decided to try our luck. With our bows packed we drove most of the night to the so-called promised land.

Hunting clear-cuts requires extensive searching for game. (Photo credit: J. Wayne Fears)

The next morning we were all stalking around our designated areas like a bunch of Indians. Needless to say, our luck was not good and the temperature was heating up. Hot temperatures are nothing uncommon for the early days of southern archery season. With the increasing heat, I soon decided to return to camp.

On my way back to camp, I encountered a large copperhead snake slithering along an abandoned road bed. Shortly after the encounter, I was traveling the road with the snake's skin in my day pack. While I was thinking about the hatband the snake was going to provide, something dawned on me. "What was the old road doing in the middle of a pine forest?" Being a little curious by nature, I began exploring the road. Shortly after, I discovered one of the most used deer trails I'd ever seen. The trail was apparent where it crossed the road. With this discovery, I quickly began following the trail into the tangle of pine trees.

Within twenty-five yards of the thicket, I discovered the remains of an old abandoned farmhouse. From the charred remnants I could tell it had burned when the clear-cut had been developed. Approximately ten yards from the house was the remains of another old building. What I saw within this building was shocking. At first I could not believe this was where the deer trail had ended. With other smaller trails appearing from other directions, I realized the old building was the center of attraction.

Copperhead snakes are frequently found by southern bow hunters. (Photo credit: Scott Shupe)

Upon entering the building, I quickly realized the reason for attraction–*salt*! There before me was one of the largest salt licks I had ever seen. It was now apparent to me that the building had been the farm's smokehouse.

Smokehouses are designated buildings used to preserve meat, which is done by placing large amounts of salt on it. It was quite apparent that the building had been around for many years, and a lot of salt had slipped through the many cracks of its floor. With this discovery I immediately began forming my hunting strategy. I would intercept the deer in the clearing of the old smokehouse to ensure a clear shot.

In short time, I had my portable tree stand in place and returned to camp. In camp I informed my friends that deer steaks were on the menu and to prepare themselves. After some joking, I returned to the stand and allowed eight deer to pass by before darkness descended upon me.

The following morning I was in position with dawn's first light. Like the evening before, I allowed several does and a small buck to pass by safely. Shortly after allowing the small buck to pass, I allowed a handsome eight point buck to enter the clearing. The buck's actions proved to be his last, as my aim was perfect.

Since that time I have learned to investigate all areas that could hold a secret. When hunting a strange area it is always wise to locate abandoned farm sites; you just never know!

Turning On During The Turnoffs

There is a phenomenon that can cause a serious deer hunter to lose a lot of sleep. The phenomenon is what I term the "whitetail turnoff." During these periods it seems like every deer in the area has left for the next zip code. One day they are there, the next day they are *gone*! In most cases it only appears that the deer have left the area. To the skilled and thinking hunter, it is just another aspect of hunting that has to be dealt with.

This is why it is important for the hunter to understand what conditions exist during the time of hunting. Factors such as food, weather, hunting pressure, rut phase, moon phase, etc., influence the existing conditions within the given habitat. With this information, veteran hunters understand how much of the animal's habits are determined by the habitat; therefore, it is during the period of a factor change that hunters could encounter a turnoff.

Wind is a disturbing factor to deer. The movement created by wind simply makes deer nervous and difficult to hunt. Basically, wind is a real pain and decreases the odds for success. But even with decreasing odds, there is always a chance for success for a thinking hunter.

During windy conditions, I love to hunt clear-cuts. The reason is simple: Clear-cuts provide both food and visibility for the deer. This is important due to the animal's sight becoming its primary defense in windy weather. Though the deer will not be as active as normal, they

Abandoned farm sites can become hunting paradises to the thinking hunter.

During windy conditions, deer are not as active as they normally are, but they can be taken.

will move to some degree. This is the reason stand sites located near heavy cover should produce better. In a nutshell, wind, such as all elements in nature, is a natural occurrence to the deer. Seasoned hunters know this and adjust to the given circumstances.

Peaking On The Peak

One of the phenomenon that upsets hunters annually is what I term the "peak-of-the-rut turnoff." This is the sudden period when deer seem to simply disappear. This turnoff is identified when the majority of scrapes and primary trails appear to have been abandoned. This occurrence may last for only a few days or extend into weeks, depending on various factors.

One such factor influencing this turnoff is hunting pressure. Hunting pressure is simply the amount of human activity within a given area. Deer know they must avoid humans and human situations to survive. Therefore, the animals seek areas that will provide protection against the existing condition. Extreme hunting pressure may result in the deer becoming nocturnal in some areas.

Dealing With Vampire Bucks

People ask me all the time, 'How do you deal with nocturnal deer?' After many years of experiencing the nocturnal turnoff, I have not discovered a foolproof technique yet. Personally, I feel it is almost impos-

Bucks such as these learn quickly to use the cover of darkness.

sible to predict what an animal will do during this stressful condition. But it is this slim chance that keeps us persistent hunters in the field, trying to unravel the mysteries of nocturnal bucks.

The value of being persistent paid off a few years ago when I was dealing with a case of nocturnal deer. For nearly a week, the numerous scrapes surrounding my stand site were totally abandoned by their creators. With the exception of a small four pointer and a few does, my many hours of hunting were fruitless. Deciding to experiment, I placed some estrous doe urine in one of the scrapes before calling it a day. Now I could only wait until morning.

The next morning, I placed a Feather Flex decoy approximately ten yards from the treated scrape. After placing the decoy, I inspected the scrape and found numerous fresh tracks indicating a deer had visited it during the night. The rest of the day was spent viewing only the dummy deer and a couple of hunters.

With darkness closing in, I retrieved the decoy and treated the scrape again. This time I incorporated the estrous doe urine with a hearty dose of buck urine. My reason for the buck urine was to leave the impression an invading buck had intercepted the doe. If my theory worked, the scrape's creator would become more protective toward his territory.

The first four hours of the following morning were spent gazing at the decoy. The midmorning ritual of hunters returning to their camps was signaled by the barking of gray squirrels. The noisy rodents con-

The use of a premium buck lure can increase a hunter's odds tremendously. (Photo credit: Sharon Haley)

tinued their calling until the hunters had vacated the area.

The woods were silent as the brilliant sun began defrosting my chilled body. The relaxation was brief as the rustling leaves cut the silence. For a long time I listened to the rhythm of the noise before deciding to move. Realizing the sounds were behind me, I slowly began looking over my right shoulder. Now my ears would guide me through the underbrush to locate the polished antlers of the buck.

A surge of excitement raced through me as the buck materialized from the undergrowth. For several seconds, the buck stood still and faced the direction of the scrape. Like a statue, the buck stood frozen in its tracks before slowly moving forward. Ever so slowly did the buck walk toward the scrape with its ears erect. Realizing the deer would soon be in front of me, I began raising my rifle. My actions were quickly halted as the buck suddenly stopped and began raising its tail upward.

For a brief second, I feared the buck was about to attempt escape. My reaction to the deer's movement was quick. Instantly I placed the crosshairs of a Simmon's scope on the buck's shoulder and fired. The shot marked a special occasion for me. I had taken one of my all-time big bucks. Due to its habits, I harvested what I felt was an almost unkillable buck. But still the question existed: Was this the buck who had been doing the night deeds? I do not know the answer to this question, and never will. To be perfectly honest, I don't want to know. I feel if I learn everything, the fun of hunting will be gone.

Thinking About The Thinking Hunter

What is a thinking hunter? Is it someone who has more knowledge about hunting? Do they have some way of receiving the thoughts of the game they pursue? Are they some kind of super-hunter who always gets their game? I truly do not think so!

Personally, I view a thinking hunter as a dedicated and caring individual: Someone who enjoys the outdoors and the sport of hunting, as well as someone who wishes the best for their fellow hunters and the future of the sport of hunting.

My interpretation of a thinking hunter is a person who thinks about what they are doing at all times. A thinking hunter is a person who

Bill Bynum feels the future of hunting is in the hands of today's hunters. His most valued memories are of hunting with his son who is an accomplished hunter himself.

uses his or her brain before ever firing a shot. A thinking hunter is someone who respects the land and understands the importance of ethical hunting.

A thinking hunter is a sportsman who strives to share the sport with those less fortunate who are not given the opportunity to enjoy the many pleasures hunting has to offer. It is these same people who will determine the future of our sport for generations to come. The people I refer to are our children, our nephews and nieces, and our neighbors' children. You never know how long the memories will last during a day afield with a child. Think about it!

Chapter 7

Senderos and Power Lines

Larry L. Weishuhn

The briars and underbrush were so thick that I was beginning to wonder if indeed I had made a wise decision in hunting the thicket. According to the local hunters the area held several good bucks, the kind I had come a long way to hunt. Try as I may I could not find a place to sit where I could see more than a few feet in any direction. By then, my hands and face were so scratched they looked like a bloody road map. Finally I found a spot where I could see about 20 feet in one direction. I sat down, waited a few minutes and started a rattling sequence. Immediately a buck responded, but the brush was so thick I could not see him. He circled my position, walked downwind and caught my scent. The next thing I heard was the sound of a big buck bounding through the underbrush and thicket.

I knew to do any good, I was going to have to find a place where I could see any deer that approached. That did not appear like it was going to be easy. I literally crawled out of the thicket on my hands and knees, then started looking for an old logging road that might cut through the thicket. In Texas we would call such a road or pathway a sendero. Having arrived only a little while before, there had been no time to scout the area I hoped to hunt. Neither had I been able to find a topographic or aerial map. Walking back toward where I had parked my vehicle, I wondered if there might be a pipeline or power line right-of-way that traversed the area.

After finding my pickup, the next couple of hours I drove around and found an old power line right-of-way. While quite often these are cleared of brush and trees, this one was not, or at least it had been a long time since it had been cleared. While the vegetation was extremely thick it was only about waist high in most areas. After parking my pickup I headed down the power line. Several deer trails crossed it. I also found several rubs and scrapes along the edges. I continued along the right-of-way until I came to an old white oak tree. Although most of its acorns had long since been eaten by deer, turkeys, and other wildlife, the old tree provided a commanding view of the power line's pathway through the dense thicket.

Utility right-of-ways that cut through dense thickets are ideal places to ambush southern whitetails.

When Do Southern Deer Move?

By then it was about midmorning. While the early morning had been extremely cold, typical of southern hunting weather, it was starting to warm up. Past experience told me southern deer do not always move much in the early morning when it is extremely cold. They wait until midmorning or even midday to become active. With this in mind I crawled into the tall oak tree.

I had been in the tree less than ten minutes when the first deer appeared. It moved slowly to the edge of the opening and peered both left and right, then started cautiously across. The little buck looked to be a good yearling, as indicated by his rack and his slender body. He continued across the nearly 40-foot wide opening and quickly disappeared into the dense thicket on the opposite side. My finding the old power line right-of-way was already starting to pay off.

The next deer to venture through the relatively open area seemed not unlike a parade of deer. From my perch I could see three different trails. Quite often there were deer crossing on all three at the same time. Most of the deer I saw were does and fawns, and an occasional young buck. By noon I had seen a total of 22 deer. Originally my intention had been to hunt until noon and then head back to camp for lunch, but with deer moving I hated to leave my "grandstand seat" high in the old oak tree. During a lull in the action I dug around in my day pack and found two candy bars and a small thermos of coffee. Not your gourmet or healthi-

An ideal aid for finding and seeing deer, even in southern woods, is the binocular.

est of meals, but certainly enough to carry me through the middle of the day and into the evening hunt.

No sooner had I unwrapped a candy bar and was about to take a bite than a decent eight point appeared on the crossing about 75 yards away. He was fairly massive and had extremely long back tines approaching 13 inches. However, his front tines were only about five inches long. When he turned to look my way, I guessed his spread to be about 17 inches. A pretty good buck, and certainly tempting. But it was the first day of a four-day hunt and I suspected there were several bucks of his caliber in the area and possibly even a few bigger.

The buck disappeared into the opposite side of the opening. It was about 30 minutes later when another buck appeared, this one a 10 point with about a 15-inch spread and not very long tines. I watched him nibble on the tips of brush as he walked slowly across the open area. Just as he reached the opposite side, he moved off of the trail and walked to one of the scrapes I had spotted while walking into the area. After freshening the scrape, he too disappeared.

All around me squirrels were busy scampering up trees, fussing at each other, and chasing one another. A couple crawled close, but then went about their own way. Suddenly, I heard a squirrel starting to fuss, and then a jay began his nagging cry. Using my binocular I watched as a coyote crept out of the underbrush, exactly downwind of where I had hung a plastic film container holding a piece of cotton doused with doe-in-heat scent. As I watched the coyote trotted directly to it. He looked around to see if anything was watching, then jumped up and grabbed the container in his mouth. Chewing on it, he disappeared again into the brush. Previously I witnessed this type of behavior by coyotes on numerous occasions while hunting in Georgia, as well as in Texas and Mexico.

The afternoon passed quickly as I was entertained by the area's wildlife. Throughout the day deer, turkeys, coyotes, and other animals put on a spectacle.

Late in the day, with the light fading quickly, what wind there was early had died down to a mere wisp. From a distance I could hear an animal walking through the dry leaves and underbrush. I imagined it being a huge buck as the sound grew louder. Impatiently I waited for "it" to appear in the low brush right-of-way. I trained and strained looking through my binocular to where I thought the deer would appear. Even though the distance was not great, I have long since found binoculars to be a great aid in helping me see more clearly, even in thick cover. The optics also help in distinguishing the size of antlers, or even picking out an antler in a mass of brush and tangle.

I watched in awe as a huge, massive-antlered buck appeared. It looked as if his bases were nearly six inches in circumference and he had a lot of points. He was definitely a shooter. I dropped my binocular and quickly replaced it with my Thompson/Center Contender carbine, chambered for the .375 Winchester, topped with a Simmons variable scope. Unfortunately, all I could see was the deer's left eye and part of his rack–not an ideal target. My increased heartbeat caused the crosshairs to bounce all over where the deer stood, even though his body was completely covered by trees and brush. I felt a severe case of buck fever coming on. I nearly got tickled at myself for the excitement I felt at seeing this deer. Many years of hunting whitetails throughout North America had not dulled the excitement I felt at seeing a monstrous whitetail. All I needed now was a chance at a shot. The buck started to move forward and I got ready. Just as quickly he stopped, turned, and disappeared into the wall of trees and brush. I watched the same area until it was totally dark, but he never reappeared. At least I knew I was in a good area for big bucks, and I had seen him. Had I been hunting in the thicket itself, I doubt seriously that I would have ever seen him or the other deer observed that day. Thankfully there would be tomorrow.

A Missed Opportunity

Early the following morning I was back in my same oak tree. At first light a small buck strode across the narrow opening. A few minutes later two does and two fawns walked across as well. No other deer came by until just before noon. I was considering getting out of the tree to stretch for a little while and then crawl back up to finish out the day. As I started crawling out of the tree, at the most inopportune time, he appeared. Before I could recover, he walked quickly across the opening and disappeared into the dense woods on the other side of the power line right-of-way. It was as if he knew what I was going to do even before I did! Talk about frustration! I hunted hard for the buck over the next four days, but never saw him again. I suppose it was something I should have suspected; big mature bucks seldom give you long to see them and then react. When they do appear, you had better be ready to take advantage of the situation. I had not been ready. As a result I missed an opportunity at one of the best bucks I had ever seen in the South.

Power line and pipeline right-of-ways serve as ideal places to plant various deer forages, such as clovers, peas, beans, and the like. These areas are easily planted and maintained and are rather long and narrow food plots that deer seem to favor over larger blocks of forages.

It was on such a narrow food plot that former Atlanta Falcon's quarterback great Steve Bartkowski took an extremely fine 10 point in Georgia. The season had only recently begun when he set up a ladder blind on a pipeline right-of-way. Shortly after daylight the buck appeared in the food plot to check on the estrus status of several does feeding there. It took only a brief moment for "Bart" to make his decision. Moments later he approached a good three-year-old buck, taken squarely through the shoulders with his Browning Stainless Stalker chambered for a .270 Winchester.

Regardless of where in the South and Southeast you hunt, there are normally utility right-of-ways. These are usually "maintained" to keep the brush and trees at a low level. As mentioned, these are also frequently planted with forage plant for deer, turkey, and other wildlife. Hunting these, especially on trails that cross them, can lead to taking a good buck.

Glenn Weishuhn checks out a utility right-of-way that serves as an excellent place to plant food plots.

The Brush Country of South Texas in some ways is similar to the dense forests and underbrush of the South and Southeast. The area is comprised of dense stands of brush that, in places, is almost impenetrable. Until oil exploration started in the region, large tracts of land were not accessible other than by foot or on horseback. As roads were cleared through the large ranches to accommodate seismograph crews, it opened much of the country to hunters. Locally these straight roads, fenceline right-of-ways, and the like are known as "senderos," which is Spanish for essentially any wide pathway through dense stands of brush. Normally these are seldom wider than 30 feet or so, and in most instances they are considerably narrower.

Deer tend to travel these senderos. Like people, deer often take the path of least resistance. Thus senderos are ideal places to ambush deer, either as they cross them or as they travel up and down the pathways. This also makes senderos ideal places in which to find rubs and especially scrapes. Quite often these are also the only open places in large, dense stands of thorn bushes and cactus.

I find senderos to be excellent places to hunt for white-tailed deer. Several of the bucks I have taken in South Texas have been taken as they crossed senderos or as they walked in them through dense thickets.

Scouting senderos to determine where to set up a tripod or ground blind is relatively easy. Simply walk in the sendero until you find a place where there are several active crossings, or scrapes. There, set up a tripod or ground blind, being sure you are downwind of such trails.

Of Senderos And Drop-tines

While hunting on the Brown Ranch near Batesville, Texas, field-testing a new Weatherby rifle, I spent several days sitting in a ground blind in an area where previously there had been spotted an old drop-tine buck. He had been seen a total of two times during the last three years. Not necessarily an established pattern. After visiting with the ranch owner, I decided the best place to hunt for this particular deer would be on a narrow sendero that passed through the dense thicket where we thought the buck might live.

I set up a ground blind on a sendero that was only about 20 feet wide, but it stretched the length of the thicket. It was the only place where I would be able to see any amount of country. Just beyond the edge of the sendero the dense thorn bushes were so thick the only way I could get through them was to crawl on my hands and knees.

The first day I hunted the ground blind I saw 10 different bucks and four does. Four of the bucks I spotted were big 10 pointers, some with spreads beyond 20 inches. But the big eight point with a drop was not among them. For the next three days I hunted the blind from nearly daylight to dark. I saw a lot of bucks, including three that sorely tempted me, but they did not quite measure up to the drop-tine buck. Had I simply been hunting for an eight or 10 point buck, the hunt could have been over minutes into the first day.

Numerous bucks made their way up and down and across the sendero on which I was sitting, hidden behind a natural brush blind. Several stopped along the edge and either opened or freshened scrapes. That is how I finally got a chance to see the drop-tine buck.

Whitetails quite often make rubs along the edge of senderos and right-of-ways.

Highly mobile tripods are ideal for hunting along the edges of senderos.

Before daylight a buck appeared in my sendero, not 20 steps from where I sat. He freshened a scrape, then walked back and forth across the sendero. Sometimes he would disappear in the thick brush for over 10 minutes, but then would reappear either a little farther away or a little closer. Unfortunately all this was in gray light, too dark to be certain it was the buck I was hunting for. I thought it probably was, but it was simply too dark to tell for sure.

Finally it got light enough to see for sure if it was the drop-tine buck. I reacted quickly by raising the new Weatherby, chambered for the .270 Winchester. When the crosshairs of the Simmons variable settled on the deer's shoulder, I squeezed the trigger. The buck fell and never moved a muscle. I ran the 185 steps to where he lay in the middle of the sendero. He was one of those bucks that had a lot of character. He was not overly wide, only about 20 inches on the main beam. He was not all that tall. His back tine lengths were eight and 10 inches, with front tines of three and two inches. Score-wise he would not have been much better than about 125 Boone and Crockett. But what really set him apart was his five-inch drop-tine, and the fact that several hunters had hunted him in the past–thankfully unsuccessfully. He was certainly a special deer, and one that I would have never taken had it not been for the sendero that cut through the dense stands of thorn bush. Neither would I have been successful had I not been persistent. It is persistence that often is the one real reason for successfully hunting a big deer.

Sendero hunting and utility right-of-way hunting in the Southeast also are conducive to still-hunting. By taking advantage of the wind in your face and the sun at your back, a hunter can slip along quietly. Were it not for such senderos, still-hunting in many areas of the South and Southwest would be impossible.

Take A Dummy Hunting

Hunting senderos sometimes takes a bit of innovation. Bucks quite often tend to cross a sendero, or for that matter a utility right-of-way, at one place for a few days and then move up or down the cut through the

Larry Weishuhn approaches the old eight point drop-tine he took in South Texas as it stood in a sendero.

Larry Weishuhn has taken many bigger bucks, but few were more satisfying than this buck he took with the aid of a mannequin.

brush or woods to cross somewhere else the next day. Quite often when I hunt senderos I do so using highly mobile tripod stands. These can be quickly positioned to take advantage of available cover, while still allowing the user to be able to see quite a few deer. Occasionally deer become wise to tripods or semi-permanent stands and cross just beyond shooting range. Such was the case with a buck I hunted for a time. The mature deer seemed to have a second sense in knowing where I was going to set up my tripod on the fenceline sendero he regularly crossed.

The first time I saw him, I knew he was a buck I wanted to take. A ranch hand spotted him crossing a sendero, and told me where he had seen the deer. During the period of a week he saw the deer several times at the same crossing. When he told me about it, I set up a tripod about 150 yards downwind of where he regularly crossed. On my initial hunt I saw the deer only momentarily. All I could see of him was his head and neck poking out of the brush, looking both ways to see if there was danger. Even though I was well camouflaged, as was my tripod, the deer spotted me immediately. I watched in amazement as he simply backed up and disappeared. Twenty minutes later I watched him cross the sendero about 400 yards away. The following day the same thing happened again. That night I moved the tripod to within about 200 yards of where the buck crossed the day before. I was confident this time he would be mine. But alas, I was wrong again. As earlier, the buck showed up about the same time as the days before, again peered in my direction with only his head and rack exposed. Upon seeing me he quickly backed up, disappeared and then about 10 minutes later reappeared about 350 yards from my tripod and crossed the sendero.

That night in camp, I found an old pair of camouflage coveralls (which I stuffed with hay), an old hunting hat, and finished off my homemade mannequin with a pair of smelly socks. When this chore was complete I went to bed and dreamed of big bucks.

The dawn was still only a promise when I carried the "dummy" to my tripod and set it up to look as much as possible like a hunter. Then, I backed away, made a large circuitous loop and sat down on the ground on the edge of the sendero. This spot was about a hundred yards from the trail where the day before the buck had peered up the sendero at my tripod to see if I was there. I broke off several limbs, stuck them in the ground around me and then waited.

Off in the distance coyotes announced the arrival of a new day. In the gray light I quietly and confidently waited. About an hour later I sat watching the part of the sendero between me and the trail the buck had used the day before, and the tripod. I saw movement at the edge of the sendero and used my binocular to confirm that it was indeed the buck I had hoped to fool. I quickly replaced the binocular with my .375 Winchester Contender handgun. When the crosshairs settled on the deer's shoulder about 75 yards distant, I squeezed the trigger. At the shot the deer went down.

During my years of hunting mature bucks, there have been quite a few bigger than the buck I had just taken, but few more satisfying!

Chapter 8

Pine Plantations

Bill Bynum

Pine trees and white-tailed deer have somehow always gone together. In my younger days of deer hunting I thought that, without a pine tree being around, my chances were slim for seeing a deer. Today I know better, but the pine tree can play a major role in southern deer hunting.

The reason for this is simple. In some areas of the southern United States pine trees are the predominant tree variety. This is due to many thousands of acres being planted to replace harvested hardwoods. This, in many ways, is a shame, but I look on this through the eyes of a hunter. Thousands of people look on this as survival; therefore, many southern hunters must cope with hunting in the vast pine plantations of the South.

My earliest experiences with pine tree hunting taught me some valuable lessons pertaining to deer–lessons that have served me well over the years. Without question, the greatest of these lessons has been to never underestimate the power of pines.

Southern hunters will discover there are various stages of pine tree growth across the South. Some pine forests feature tall, beautiful trees towering skyward. Within these forests deer can find excellent areas for bedding. These areas provide both shelter and visibility for the animals. It is this factor that often leads me to hunt pine forests during certain hunting conditions.

One of these conditions is heat. During periods of extreme heat deer can find comfort in the shade of the pine tree. In the early days of archery season I discovered a technique for procuring venison. I learned this technique many years before I found gray in my hair.

When It All Began

It had been an unusually hot and dry summer for the entire southeastern United States. Forest fires were being reported with alarming frequency. Walking through the woods sounded like a mouse in a box of corn flakes. In short, it was dry and just plain miserable. Much of the misery was being generated by the high levels of humidity. High humid-

Pine trees play an important role in hunting southern deer. (Photo credit: J. Wayne Fears)

ity mixed with the unseasonably warm temperatures can diminish the degree of hunting pleasure. Another existing factor was the deer were not moving much during the daylight hours. The deer were feeding in the coolness of the night under the big full moon.

With these existing conditions, few hunters were venturing afield during this time. This resulted in no animals being forced to move by hunting pressure. In short, things were pretty stagnated!

Days passed as I stood watch over a large soybean field. Every morning I listened to the sounds of fleeing deer as I ventured to my stand. Sometimes I was lucky and got a glimpse of white in the moonlight. These brief sightings were the extent of my daily encounters with the white-tailed deer.

I was now becoming discouraged. I had not pointed an arrow at a deer in four days of hunting. In fact, I saw only a couple of does, and they were well out of range of my arrows. Adding to this insult were the numerous tracks surrounding the field.

Beneath my tree stand the ground revealed that deer had been traveling heavily in the area. Staring at those tracks for hours, wishing I could see the creators, deflated my ego even more. I was determined to use my harvest tag before the week was over.

Descending from my stand one morning I decided to follow some of the beaten paths. I had an idea where they would lead, but I wanted to be sure. The trails were worn nearly bare from the nightly travel of the deer. Within an hour I had slowly traveled through a small cedar thicket and was still tracking. I was amazed to discover few of the travelers had diverted from the trails. There was no debate; the deer knew where they were going.

Soon I was standing at the edge of a large pine grove. The trees towered over undergrowth that resembled a jungle. Only the areas where the trails led gave access into the main body of the forest. The following hour was spent exploring the inside of the pine grove. After recovering a topo map from my day pack, I began studying the contours of the area. I was happy to locate the basin that sliced its way through the center of the forest. In the center of the basin the map revealed a small creek. The creek could play an important role when it came time to hunt. Things were looking better all the time!

Slowly traveling through the underbrush, I saw numerous deer beds. Upon inspecting the bedding sites I knew the deer were near. This was accomplished by placing my hand on the bed. If the bedding site felt warm I knew an animal had just recently abandoned it. Also, many times small piles of deer droppings would be at the edge of the bed. These telltale signs are always informative to the knowledgeable hunter. Upon inspection I knew many of the deer were feeding on the green soybean leaves. The only soybean field near this location was the one I was hunting.

I made my exit from the pine forest via the creek. An abundance of trails crossed the shallow stream. The clear water of the creek revealed numerous tracks where deer had stood and quenched their thirst.

While many hunters fail to use the terrain to their advantage, Bill Bynum does not.

There was no question in my mind that the creek would play a major role in my hunting strategy.

Within an hour I located the exact spot from where I wanted to hunt. The area contained an intersection of four different trails. With this number of travelways, I knew my chances of seeing deer were good!

Approximately 15 yards from the intersection I built a ground blind of small leafy bushes. (These were the days before affordable portable tree stands.) After completing the blind, I walked straight to the creek. The position of the creek was perhaps ten or so yards behind my blind. Upon reaching the creek, I pushed a large limb into the mud. The limb would serve as a marker when I returned in the dark.

Using the creek as my mode for travel allowed me to exit the pine forest quietly. This, I felt, would be a definite advantage come morning.

The next morning found me slowly wading the ankle-deep waters of the creek. I could see fairly well in the fading light of the full moon. I had replaced the batteries inside my two-celled flashlight with some that had been used. I thought weaker light would help hide my presence within the pines. I recall a few times I had wished the light was brighter to identify some crooked sticks. Snakes also have a tendency to follow creeks!

Soon I had approached the marker and was nested inside the blind. The moonlight had given way and the first signs of daylight appeared in the eastern sky. The faint call of a great horned owl disrupted the eerie silence. Time seemed to stop as my excitement intensified. I could not

Bill Bynum (left) proudly displays one of the many bucks that he has harvested from pine forests.

With the aid of a modern tree stand, hunting pine trees can be productive. (Photo credit: J. Wayne Fears)

wait for dawn so I could start hunting. I could feel the tension mounting within me as I nocked my arrow. Something exciting was going to happen, I could feel it!

Something did happen within minutes of preparing my bow. Far off behind me I heard a sound that I had never heard before in my native land. A sound that took me by surprise–the sound of coyotes greeting the morning sun. I listened in vain for the coyotes to repeat their eerie cries. Perhaps it was this distraction that allowed the deer to enter my area undetected.

With the first look at the buck I thought I was imagining its presence. Less than ten yards from me stood the most massive buck I had ever seen. The buck's rack spread several inches beyond its ears. Five tines rose high on each side as he stood facing me.

In all my years of hunting the magnificent white-tailed deer, I had never been as startled as I was at that moment. This amazement continued for several moments as I desperately tried to regain my composure. I could sense that within moments, my chance would transform into reality.

It suddenly appeared as if something forced the buck to turn his head. It was with this motion I raised my bow and began drawing the arrow. I could feel the rush of excitement flowing inside me as my fingers reached my lips. This was the anchor point of draw and I could now release the arrow. In the time it takes to blink an eye, the arrow traveled its path, a path that guided the arrow less than an inch over the back of the deer.

Perhaps it was the sounds of the fleeing deer that drowned out the sound of my arrow piercing the pine tree. Perhaps it was the shock of seeing the arrow in the tree that caused momentary paralysis within me. The thing I do know is that I will never forget that morning as long as I live.

I will also always remember the valuable lessons I learned while hunting in that pine forest–lessons that, luckily, have helped me in harvesting scores of deer from beneath tall pine trees.

Hunters will often find that other stages of pine growth can produce good hunting. Pine trees will attract deer at almost every stage of development. I have found areas containing trees averaging six to twelve feet (short pines) to be the most productive. The reason for this is that these trees provide cover for the deer. Due to the height of the trees, the tree tops create a jungle of pine needles, a jungle that can hide anything that ventures within it. This can be extremely important in areas where deer receive a high amount of hunting pressure. Deer will learn quickly that their survival may depend on them keeping clear from the eyes of hunters.

Hunters will learn quickly that hunting thick clusters of pine trees can be frustrating. Due to the lack of visibility, deer can be within mere feet of an unsuspecting hunter. Limited visibility can reverse these roles, also. Therefore, it is important for the hunter to be ready at all times when hunting under these conditions. I learned this lesson the hard way a few years ago while hunting short pines.

Hunting within the jungle of small pine trees will test hunters to the limit.

The Needle-Head Buck

For decades my favorite establishment for gathering local information has been the Coffee Cup restaurant. Within the walls of the coffee shop some bizarre hunting tales have been told. I think many of these stories were creations of a hunter's vivid imagination. Some stories proved to be true accounts as trophy buck mounts will attest.

During the mid-1980s a rumor was told of an unusual buck. The buck was supposed to have a large and odd-looking rack. The rumor was that this so-called buck supported ten or twelve long tines and doubled this number with cheaters. Cheater points, often called stickers, are small antler tines measuring less than one inch in length. Naturally this created an unusual trophy by anyone's standard. Equally natural, the buck was given the nickname of Ol' Needle Head. Ol' Needle Head had become everyone's dream and the hunt was on!

Ol' Needle Head had been seen near some public hunting grounds. The property was owned by a large paper corporation that allowed hunting. With the price of a permit fee, the vast jungle of small pines quickly became a heavily hunted area.

For weeks some of the area's best deer hunters searched the pine trees daily. Like the rest of the hunters, I would spend every minute I could hunting Ol' Needle Head. Day in and day out the hunt for Ol' Needle Head continued in vain. Some hunters tried every trick in the book to lure the legendary deer into range. Other hunters sat for hours star-

Trophy bucks such as this can exist within a pine grove and never be spotted by hunters.

ing into the wall of green pine trees, hoping the buck would appear. For almost the entire hunting season the pine grove was hunted daily. It was not until the final days of the season that Ol' Needle Head began to take on mythical proportions.

Winter was now taking its toll on the few hunters who would not give up on Ol' Needle Head. Rain, sleet, snow, freezing temperatures–you name it–greeted the remaining hunters. It was the harsh weather that finally forced all but a few of us to surrender. It was then that I began feeling I had a chance of encountering the fabled buck.

It was early on the next to the last day of the deer season that my luck changed. Huddled beneath a pine tree, I sat watching an intersection of two deer trails. The reason I chose this location was due to some massive rubs I had discovered weeks before. The trees had been violently rubbed free of their bark, and numerous limbs were broken. I knew it had taken a nice sized buck to administer the damage and hoped it was Ol' Needle Head.

The dark gray clouds of December were slowly yielding to the rising sun. My range of visibility was less than fifteen yards into the pine trees. With these factors prevailing, I was beginning to question my sanity. Here I was sitting on frozen ground hunting a buck that I was not sure even existed!

During the time of my soul searching, I failed to notice movement along the deer trail. I knew the deer had to follow the trail because deer simply do not pop up out of the ground. Either way, when I glanced up, a little four point buck was looking me in the eyes. The realization of what was happening quickly relieved me of the cold. Knowing any type of sudden movement would send the deer scurrying, I slowly began to close my eyes. With my eyes nearly closed I focused on the animal's feet and began listening closely. I knew my ears would instruct me of the activities of my surroundings. What appeared to be an eternity ended in a few short minutes as the deer slowly walked away. At this point I was really questioning my sanity! I could have used the meat the four-pointer would have provided. Now I was really frustrated at myself!

Hours passed as I sat and mentally scolded myself for even getting out of bed that morning. During this time I had seen only a few crows and a bluejay. The deer were simply not moving and I was sure I was wasting my time.

Soon I had myself convinced it was time to go and started to stand from my position. Perhaps it was the change in elevation that permitted me to see the pine tree, I do not remember. However, I do remember seeing the shape of a deer through the tangle of pine needles. Motionless, I stood waiting for the deer to move forward so I could make positive identification. If the deer proved to be a legal buck, it would be mine!

This thought had hardly cleared my brain when the deer began moving. Through the pine needles I could see the outline of the buck's rack. I slowly began raising my rifle to prepare for the shot. I knew there was little time as the buck quickened its pace.

A set of rattling antlers can be useful when hunting pines.

Hunters will learn the value of repeating guns when hunting dense pines. (Photo credit: J. Wayne Fears)

In seconds the rifle was aimed at a small opening where I knew the deer would enter. Viewing through the rifle scope, I waited for the buck to enter the crosshairs. This buck was mine and I knew it; I was confident as I released the rifle safety. It was with the snapping of the safety that I received the shock of my life.

Like the booming of thunder, the ground behind me erupted with noise, startling me. The unexpected shock sent me leaping in a state of confusion. Instantly I spun around to see the source of the disturbance. Only for a second did I see the creator of the disturbance before the pine trees engulfed it, but during that split second I clearly saw the massive rack of a buck. The long polished antler tines glowed like lighting bolts in the dark. The sight of those antlers darting into the pines will always burn in my memory. This is especially true of the many cheater points that covered the massive rack. There was no question about it, it was Ol' Needle Head!

Unknown to me is the amount of time I spent standing in total amazement and where or when the other buck escaped. I do remember questioning myself about what I had seen. I also remember asking myself if I should tell my friends. These questions haunted my thoughts throughout the night. It was these thoughts that entertained me the final day of the hunting season. It is still the memory of seeing the legendary buck people laugh about. It is this memory that guides me to pine plantations each hunting season–the pine plantations that many legendary bucks call home.

The sounds of another buck can create some explosive results when using a grunt call.

Prime Time For Pines

During the past few decades I have tried various tactics for harvesting pine tree bucks. Through these tactics I have discovered many products offered on today's market are sound investments. This is true of commercial grunt callers. Though I have explained the use of grunt callers in Chapter 10, this is additional information that I feel could make a difference when hunting in thick pines.

During the periods of pre-rut and post-rut, bucks are aggressive towards each other. This is due to the low amount of estrous does within the area. The sounds of a buck tending a doe can quickly bring another buck from its domain, the reason I like to slowly stalk pine groves during these rutting periods.

Slowly moving into the wind and producing two or three calling sequences can be lethal on deer. This is a method for luring bucks to within mere feet of the hunter. The key is for the hunter to be alert and expect the unexpected. Learning to expect the unexpected is what transforms legendary bucks into trophies!

Chapter 9

Using Scents

Bill Bynum

I can remember the days before commercial deer lures ever hit the sporting goods stores. The funny thing is, I'm not that old!

I remember the first bottle of commercial deer lure I ever bought. I was so excited knowing this magic potion was the answer to all my deer hunting problems that I could hardly sleep the night before I poured all my allowance on the frosty ground. My disappointment was greater

Today there are many products found within the commercial scent industry. Bill Bynum believes they increase the hunter's success rate when used properly.

Applying the proper scent at the correct time can make dreams come true.

than the fatigue the next day. The only deer I saw nearly turned inside out running from my secret weapon.

Decades have passed since that day and many lessons have been learned pertaining to commercial lures. I would also like to mention that many deer have dropped while learning these lessons.

For several years I have worked in various capacities within the commercial scent industry. My duties have been everything from research to marketing, product development, and lecturing on hunting with scents. From all my involvement over the years with commercial scents, one thing is clear: I will not go deer hunting without them for the reasons we are about to explore.

I have become a firm believer in certain aspects of deer hunting. One such aspect is that deer communicate with scent more than any other form of communication. Another aspect pertaining to the subject is the olfactory capabilities of deer. Their olfactory capabilities are many times greater than that of humans.

I also believe many hunters fail to respect the animal's intelligence level. For instance, some hunters defeat their purpose when applying commercial scents. These hunters are using commercial scents like they were a lucky rabbit's foot. They'd be better off playing lotto. To better explain this, let's review some important elements pertaining to commercial lures and their applications.

As stated previously, there are a lot of commercial scent products on the market today. Most of these products will aid the hunter in luring animals. I feel the problem many hunters have with using scents is that they do not use the proper type of lure at the proper time. Hunters must remember that during the hunting season, the habits of the deer are changing.

During the early days of the bow season the bachelor groups of the summertime are dissolving. The mature bucks are trying to establish their territories for the upcoming breeding season. In most cases, this will occur weeks before the does come into the estrous cycle. This is why it is important for the hunter to use the proper type of attractant for a given time period; therefore, we should see the importance of timing and using commercial scents.

The Basic Lures

Basically, when dealing with commercial lures there are two categories. The first category is the *attractors*. These are the types that will lure the deer to the hunter. The second category of commercial scents is the *cover* scents. Cover scents are those that disguise the hunter's scent from the deer. We will discuss these products later in the chapter. First let's review the attractors.

The Attractors

Today most commercial attractors are those that are produced from deer *urine*. When we purchase a bottle of this type of lure we are simply buying deer urine, or at least we are supposed to be buying deer urine. A few years ago there were allegations of fraud among some scent companies. Today there is little to worry about from major lure producers. Among the urine-based lures, hunters will discover three common types. First, there is *estrous type* urine that represents a doe in heat. These are the products that play upon the sexual desires of a lovesick buck. Secondly, we have *nonestrous* type doe urine, or just plain doe urine. Nonestrous urines are to be used simply as a means of giving the impression that a deer was present within the given area. Thirdly, there is *buck* urine. And that's exactly what it is–buck urine. To the hunter, this type of lure may be the most lethal of all. The reason for this is it is used as an infringe-

A quality buck urine can increase the bow hunter's odds for success.

ment lure. During most hunting periods, bucks simply do not like the presence of another buck.

With these three types of lures and some knowledge, a hunter can develop a *scent hunting strategy*. But in order to develop a successful strategy, there are other factors that should also be reviewed.

Many hunters fail to understand what commercial lures really are. Of the three aforementioned lures, all are deer urines that have been placed in some form of container. So what is so important about that? Urine is high in ammonia and when stored will become even stronger smelling with time. We should know this by removing the top from our lure and taking a good sniff. In most cases the human nose has no problem detecting the scent.

Now, if the human nose can detect the scent, how do you think the nose of a deer will detect it? Common sense should tell us that the deer will receive the scent message many times greater than the human.

For years, various scent producers instructed hunters to use the concentrated lure in the same manner we would use fresh urine. Fresh urine does not have the strong smelling odor of the concentrate! Therefore, when applying the concentrate, are we not creating an unnatural scent to the animal? I think so! I have seen native reactions when using the full strength lures. This is the reason I dilute the concentrate with spring water. By doing this, a more natural smell will develop.

Some hunters simply apply commercial scents in a haphazard way. They take the top off the bottle and pour the lure on the ground. True, this is the method some scent producers recommend. I am also sure

The nose of a trophy buck is nothing to fool with if the hunter is seeking his antlers.

this is good for scent sales, but I am not worried about selling scent. I worry about luring a deer into range of my bow. This is the reason I feel the method of application is as important as the scent itself. The method used in applying scent can vary in a number of ways.

Basically there are two modes of scent application. The first mode is a *stationary* application. This is where a scent dispenser is placed in a stationary position. Stationary positioning allows the air currents to transmit the scent molecules.

Many hunters prefer using 35mm film canisters filled with cotton for this method. This is a simple and effective method for applying scent.

When using film canisters I tape a clothespin to the canister. With the clothespin I can quickly attach the applicator to or detach the applicator from a tree limb. This method is also helpful in saving scent. The lid of the canister can be replaced and will save the lure for another time. Over the years the film canister method has lured a number of deer for me. It was this method that taught me a valuable lesson pertaining to deer hunting.

The use of 35mm film canisters is an excellent method for dispensing scent.

The lesson is to respect all the senses of deer, especially the intelligence of the animal. Like many hunters, I would get into my tree stand and hang the film canisters around me. Most of the time my tree stand would be elevated to a height of approximately fifteen feet or more.

Often the deer would enter the area and begin sniffing the air currents and, within seconds, I would be looking into the eyes of an animal just moments before it made a hasty retreat. Perhaps the deer was smelling me. Perhaps it was smelling my lure. One thing was for sure, the deer was using its nose to locate the source of the scent. This is true even at an elevated position.

Wise hunters will always remember that a deer's nose is like a magnet. Deer can detect the direction from which the scent molecules are being transmitted. It is this keen sense of smell that often defeats the hunter. The reason I mention this is many hunters place the film canister upon the ground near them. The only time scent should be dispensed at ground level is to serve as a distraction. This is important for those hunting with archery equipment.

The Difference In Broadheads And Bullets

Bowhunters should have the deer's attention focused away from them. The reason for this is that few arrows can match the speed of a deer's reflexes. To properly execute an arrow shot, the animal should be unaware of the hunter's presence. Therefore, if we lure a deer into our shooting range, we must remain undetected by the animal. This is why I place a few drops of lure upon the ground. With luck, the animal will briefly focus its attention to the ground and away from me.

Placing the scent at ground level for long-range luring will somewhat reduce the odds for success. This is due to the scent not being transmitted as far by the air currents. Remember that it will be the air currents that carry the scent molecules.

Today hunters can purchase battery-powered scent dispensers that are supposed to cast scent. This is accomplished by a small fan or some other mechanical device. Some of these "scent senders" also heat the lure to make it even more appealing. Having used a few of these devices I feel the money can be spent more wisely, but to each his own!

Perhaps the most common form of dispensing scent is with foot pads or drag cloths. Foot pads are attached to the hunter's boot and lure is then added. Drag cloths work basically the same way as foot pads, as both apply lure to the ground. In short, it is a personal preference.

Many of the instructions I have read over the years have instructed me to apply the scent to the applicator and travel to the hunting site. Like many hunters, I followed these instructions until the day I watched the rear end of a nice white-tailed buck following my trail.

Shortly, another deer came across my trail and proceeded in the same manner as the first had done. Perhaps the second deer was following the trail of the first. Maybe it was following mine. Either way, the deer walked away from me. As disappointed as I was for not getting a shot that morning, I was happy I had witnessed this. The reason I was happy

Bill Bynum believes the use of foot pads can be effective in luring deer.

is that I had been given a great opportunity to apply some common sense to using commercial scents. Allow me to explain.

My theory is simply this: Hunters should understand that the reason a deer follows a scent trail is to seek out the scent producer. The olfactory capabilities of deer are so great they can distinguish the direction of travel. Like a dog, a deer can trail by the amount of scent molecules from one position to another. The animals know by following the weaker scent to the stronger scent, they should find the source of the scent.

This is why I prefer the use of foot pads over drag cloths. Foot pads permit me to better place scent upon the ground. This is due to the foot pad connecting directly with the ground. I also like the convenience of easy removal from my boots. Foot pads are my favorite method when deer are actively moving about.

The technique I use for trailing is quite simple. I first allow myself some extra time at my stand site. The purpose for this is to make my scent trails. At my stand site, I apply my foot pads and scent. Then I begin walking towards the target areas. These will be designated areas of deer activity such as trails, scrapes, or rubs. While en route I avoid touching anything and try to walk as quietly as possible. Upon reaching the target, I place a film canister filled with lure high in a bush. The film canister will usually contain the same lure I have used for trailing.

The scent from the elevated canister will be distributed by the air currents. This will increase the range of the scent over the target area. If a responding deer locates the canister location it should intercept my scent trail. This technique has proven to be highly effective during the pre-rut and post-rut periods. It is during these periods I find commercial lures work best.

Now let's review another important factor pertaining to commercial scents, *communication*.

Deer Like To Communicate With Deer

Some hunters often forget why they are using a commercial lure. I'll bet if you asked them they would say they were trying to lure a deer into range. Therefore, the lure is being used as a form of communication to the animal. If the proper message has been communicated, odds for response are good. So one of the secrets is transmitting the proper message! This is where many hunters fail when using commercial scents. It is my opinion that the lure must represent a want or need of the animal before it can work and why it is important that the proper attractant be used at the right time.

The type of lure used will be determined by the period of the deer's rutting cycle. This is the reason it is important to know what the deer are doing. Knowing the actual phase of the rut is critical to successful hunting with scents. If the hunter has a good idea of the natural conditions that exist, communication is made easier. When trying to communicate with deer, the scent of another deer should be the logical lure use.

Deer use scent to communicate, and wise hunters will do the same thing.

Developing A Bow Hunting Strategy

In most states the first hunters afield are those using archery equipment. Many states allow the harvesting of both bucks and does with archery equipment. This is the reason I use only two types of lures: either nonestrous doe urine or buck urine, and this is due to the state of the rutting period. During the early days of archery season few, if any, does are in the estrous cycle. Deer know what is transpiring within their habitat. Therefore, anything unnatural to the area is alarming to the animal.

At Home In The Woods

I believe the more natural the area, the more relaxed the deer should be. This is why I do not use estrous-type lures until the deer inform me to do so. By informing, I mean I will not change until I see various rutting signs appear. Signs such as scrapes, heavy rubbing activity, or single bucks and does traveling together are indications that the species are breeding. But for early hunting, and until these sign appear, I will avoid estrous-type lures.

Dissolving of the bachelor groups can usually be signaled by the rubbing of small trees. During this period bucks are beginning to prove their dominance. With the beginning of this pecking order, many younger bucks become confused. The confusion is created by the hos-

Rubs such as these are excellent indicators of a buck's presence. The scent of an estrous doe could produce quick results for the hunter.

tility of their companions and the younger bucks become lonesome and seek companionship. In short, it is a moment of weakness.

The females are also this way to some extent, so the use of the non-estrous doe urine can be applied. Wise hunters learn quickly it is these moments that increase the odds for success.

The key to using any of these attractants is knowing what phase of the reproduction cycle is taking place. Once I begin finding numerous rubs upon fair-sized trees, I begin one of my favorite game plans. In the early days of (archery) hunting season, I prefer the use of buck urine because I am trying for a buck before the hunting pressure begins. The reason I prefer this lure is the mature bucks are trying to establish personal territory. This can be identified by numerous rubs within a given area. The method I prefer to use during this phase of the rut is the *mock rub* method.

The Mock Rub

It is my opinion that many hunters fail to utilize the habits of the deer. The more natural we represent a hunting method, the better the odds of success. In preparing a mock rub I do exactly what a buck will do to some extent. I use a deer antler to rub a small tree or trees to create the visual marker. Next I place buck urine approximately four feet from the rub and leave the area.

In most cases I will allow 24 to 48 hours to expire before checking the rub site. If a buck has challenged my rubs with actual rubs, I will place a portable tree stand nearby and begin hunting. To be quite frank about the subject, I do not like to hunt anywhere there are not a few rubs present. Rubs are visual decoys that some bucks simply cannot pass up! Another method for putting meat in the freezer is the *mock-scrape* technique.

During the final days of archery season numerous scrapes will begin to appear. These scrapes are indicators that the bucks are ready for the breeding season. In most cases, the number of estrous does in the area will be low. This is exactly what the hunter wants when applying a mock-scrape. With only a handful of estrous does, a lovesick buck can become quite foolish. Bucks will become more active during the first signs of breeding.

A mock-scrape is easily made by simply locating a low hanging tree limb and kicking the debris from the ground the same way that a deer would do. Then place the scent of both a buck and an estrous doe inside the mock-scrape. This system works as an infringement upon the buck's territory. In some cases this technique has helped me in collecting deer that were moving in a nocturnal pattern.

In summary, if love is on a buck's mind, nothing else matters!

Scents And The Peak

Without question, most hunters have their greatest success during the *peak* of the rut. The peak is the time period when the majority of the females are in the estrous cycle. This is the time frame the bucks have been waiting for. It is also the period most hunters have been waiting for.

Bucks such as this one can be taken when the hunter applies natural methods for luring.

In the southern regions this time frame coincides with the primary gun season. This is the reason so many bucks fail to see the following hunting seasons. So if this is the best time to hunt deer, what is the best lure to use?

During the peak of the rut a lure will have little, if any, value to the hunter. It is simply too difficult for any lure to compete with *Mother Nature*. Trying to trick a buck into following a single source with so many does in estrus is almost impossible. But there have been a few times during the peak I have had bucks follow my scent trail. It is simply a game of odds in my opinion. Though the odds are slim for a response, they are even slimmer if there is no scent trail at all! Remember that the bucks are seeking out all the does they can find during this time frame. This is why I use a quality brand doe-in-estrous lure.

When using estrous-type lures, I do not dilute the lure as much as I normally would. In most cases, the blend will be one-third ounce water to one ounce of commercial urine. The reason for this is deer may not smell as well in colder temperatures as they do in warmer temperatures. Like humans, deer must have moisture to allow the sinus passages to function normally. This is the purpose for using commercial humidifiers in our homes. Animals use the saliva from their tongues to keep their noses moist. With this information we should know hunting during periods of low humidity is best.

It is during these periods I use one of my favorite techniques of scrape hunting. This technique requires using estrous doe urine in conjunction with buck urine. The method I prefer is to simply place both types of lures inside the scrape.

I use one type of lure on one foot pad, another type of lure on the other foot pad to make my scent trail. This has proven to be a good method when hunting in extremely heavy cover.

Hunting The Post-Rut

Hunting the post-rut is a subject that has filled the pages of numerous magazines. In most cases the lessons received pertaining to the subject are complex. Personally, I find nothing complex about hunting the post-rut. Actually it is nothing more than hunting the pre-rut with fewer bucks to respond. In the final days of hunting season, a high percentage of the season's bucks are resting in someone's deep freezer. This means the hunter must hunt deer that have become wise to the hunter.

When hunting the post-rut, my preferred technique is hunting an active scrape. When I mention the word hunting, I mean spending every available minute I can at the scrape.

The technique that has paid big dividends has been using a doe deer decoy near the scrape. This has provided me with some real thrills while watching deer respond to the decoy.

There are a few things that can increase the odds for success. Cover scents are one such thing that will help. I will discuss the use of cover scents in Chapter 12.

Chapter 10: Part I

Calling Southern Deer: Vocalizations

Bill Bynum

Hours had passed since I had taken my hunting position. During this time I had witnessed two squirrels feeding upon the ground. Apparently the game was not moving this morning. It was also apparent I was becoming chilled and bored.

My mind now wandered to many of life's mysteries as I sat staring at the buck rub. The rub was located approximately 20 yards in front of me. Five yards to the right of the rub was a fresh buck scrape. The appearance of the scrape was noticeable to my eyes. The darkness of the black dirt among the fallen leaves presented some form of excitement within me.

Perhaps this excitement was being generated by my imagination, as I was envisioning a heavy-antlered buck standing in the scrape. I imagined the sights of my shotgun centered squarely upon the buck's shoulder. It was these mental pictures that kept me glued to the frozen ground.

Time passed and I began thinking of some hot coffee. Actually, I was thinking about anything more comfortable than what I was doing. Maybe it was my imagining that caused me to focus on something other than coffee.

Somehow my ears intercepted a strange sound. I wasn't sure what I had heard, so I concentrated on every sound available. Noises such as wind, rustling leaves, and my stomach growling were obvious. Then I realized my stomach was not growling!

Long moments ticked by as I strained my hearing in vain for another clue. While I waited, I began to think I had only heard the creaking of tree. My thoughts suddenly changed when I heard the guttural sounds again. This time I distinguished the sound.

I shifted my eyes to my left, where I had heard the noises. Now both my eyes and ears located the source of the sounds. With my senses locked on the location, my mind quickly became boggled. There before me stood a sleek six-point buck that produced another series of sounds.

Bill Bynum has successfully used commercial deer callers for many years.

To this day I cannot recall ever raising the shotgun or releasing the gun's safety. I can remember the deer producing another guttural series of "grunts" as I took aim. I can also remember the scope on the deer and hearing the grunts before the sound of the gun blast. Little did I know the sounds my youthful ears had received that morning would inspire me for decades to come.

The Ever Important Grunt Caller

More than two decades have passed since I first used a commercial deer caller. During these years I have seen many bucks drop while responding to a deer "grunter." I have also witnessed numerous deer quickly leave the area! It has been these negative results that have influenced me the most. This is due to my curiosity of why an animal does what it does.

Like most hunters, I enjoy all aspects of hunting, but it is the positive aspects I relish the most. To receive these positive results, I feel numerous negative aspects must be experienced before knowledge can be gained.

In game calling, various factors must be mastered before positive results will occur. These factors will determine the outcome of a hunt. Some of the factors I refer to are improper calling locations, nonreceptive animals, or improper calling technique! Personally, I think the latter is the most common error linked to calling deer.

Many hunters feel they are buying instant success when purchasing a deer call. Sorry, it's not that simple. There are some important elements to successful deer calling, some of which a few hunters fail to realize.

One such element is knowledge of the animal's vocalization. Like any language, each sound has a meaning. This is the reason it is important to understand the various vocalization patterns of the animal. Without this knowledge we are creating an unknown situation to the deer. It would be like someone speaking a foreign language to you!

Learning the various sounds is not as difficult as it used to be. Today hunters can learn the meaning of various deer sounds in the privacy of their homes. This is due to the modern VCR player and audio cassette player. With these devices hunters can watch or listen to leading authorities explain the meanings of various sounds. In most cases, these authorities have done extensive research in the field to gain their knowledge. Sadly, many important elements are not included because of the required length of these programs. Therefore, I will cover some of the key factors many programs leave out. Among these points, *rut phase* is a critical element. Basically there are three phases of the rut: the *pre-rut, peak rut*, and *post-rut* phases.

Pre-rut is the period when only a small percentage of the does begin the estrous cycle. This phase of the rut can usually be determined by the increase of noticeable *buck scrapes*. Why is this information important to successful calling?

Buck scrapes are territorial markers created by the bucks. These areas are made by the animal simply pawing away debris and urinating upon

Bill Bynum displays one of many trophy bucks lured by a grunt call.

When bucks begin making scrapes it is time to use grunt calls regularly while hunting.

the scrape. This serves as the buck's personal signpost. These signposts inform other deer of the buck's presence and are important to a hunting strategy.

Locating scrapes should cause the hunter to take quick action. This action can be triggered quickly with the aid of a commercial grunt call. Bucks often become vocal when approaching or are at the site of a scrape. This informs any animals near the scrape of his arrival. The vocalization at this time is usually low in volume. The length of the grunting will consist of four to seven notes. This can be duplicated easily with a commercial grunt caller. Sounds simple, doesn't it! In reality, it is. It is some of the common mistakes hunters make that result in unsuccessful hunting.

Here are a few tips on using a commercial deer caller that will pay off:

*** Never call to an animal that is looking towards you. Remember the eyes and ears of a deer are keen. A deer can pinpoint the exact location from where the sound was produced.

*** Do not overcall. When using a "Buck Grunter," produce approximately five to seven quick grunts and quit! This is the normal series a buck creates.

*** Maintain proper positioning. Try to position yourself where the deer cannot see beyond you. Remember, if a deer hears another deer, it expects to see another deer! This is the reason I like using one of the modern deer decoys when hunting near scrapes.

The use of fawn bleats can aid bow hunters. Note the hunters positioning for concealment while calling.

By positioning the decoy slightly behind and to the side of you, the buck will not focus on you. This can be important to archery hunters, as well as the gun hunter.

The Fawn Bleat Caller

The fawn bleat caller is perhaps one of the least used of the commercial deer callers. The reason is the majority of deer hunters hunt during the winter months. During the winter, most fawns have lost their spots and have a different appearance. These yearlings have been sent on their way into the world by mommy. Therefore, the parental bond has been broken and little, if any, response will be given. On the other hand, archery hunters can make good use of these callers. Most southern bow hunters are afield while some of the late-born fawns are still clinging to mommy. This parental bond can produce quick response for the hunter using a fawn bleat caller.

During this time of parental bonding, hunters should use extreme caution. When utilizing a fawn bleat caller, it must be remembered that some does may still be nursing fawns. In most instances, nursing does will have the fawns nearby for reference. One indicator of a "wet doe" is body appearance. Often a nursing doe will have the appearance of weight loss- -or what we southerners term "Poor Looking." Another indicator of a wet doe is the extended nipples from her udder. This can be visible to the hunter's eyes at close range at ground level. With this information, we can determine that using a fawn bleat call can be a risky deal. The good news is the males will often respond!

When using a fawn bleat caller, I prefer to use it sparingly. I also avoid using it in a highly distressed manner. This helps eliminate some of the possibilities of calling a wet doe.

The method I prefer is using a couple low volume "bleats" to do the job. When using the bleat caller in a relaxed and soft volume manner, it represents a contact call. A contact call is nothing more than a vocalization deer use to allow each other to know where they are.

Hunters should take note of the natural volume of game vocalization. In many cases, the volume animals produce is much lower than hunters imitate. Imitating the natural volume level is important to successful calling. The more natural the sound, the better. Hunters should remember the hearing ability of deer is greater than humans; therefore, what may sound natural to us will be too loud to the animal.

Hunters who practice this regimen and follow the tips I have given should find little, if any, difficulty in calling deer.

Chapter 10: Part II

Calling Southern Deer: Rattling

Larry L. Weishuhn

To me there is no more exciting way to attract a whitetail than by using rattling horns to imitate the sounds of two bucks sparring or fighting. Exactly why white-tailed bucks spar and fight is not really important, but there are numerous explanations. Some experts think they fight over territory, yet a white-tailed buck is not truly territorial. Some say bucks fight over does, yet more often than not, there are not any does even close when two bucks engage in combat. Still others say bucks fight and spar to establish dominance or to reassure dominance. I personally suspect the latter comes closest to being the truth than any other explanation. I also believe bucks fight during the rut because their testosterone levels are extremely high. This makes them irritable. They go looking for a fight to help alleviate their anxieties. Frankly, to me it is immaterial why bucks fight or respond to rattling antlers. What is important is that bucks do fight as the rut approaches, and, the sounds of a fight often attract other bucks.

Bucks respond to rattling horns in a variety of ways. The classic response brings the buck charging in, his eyes bugged, hair standing on end to make him look even bigger and more intimidating than he is, ready to take on the world. Bucks do respond in this manner, but not nearly as often as some expert horn rattlers would have us believe. The more common response is for the buck to respond slowly and cautiously, nearly always circling downwind to try to scent the cause of the fight and ruckus. For this reason it is always a good idea to set up so you or a trusted companion can watch downwind. Sometimes the big bucks are extremely slow to respond, taking as long as 30 or more minutes to show up.

I am not always a patient horn rattler. All too often I rattle for 5 or 10 minutes, then wait an additional 20 minutes before moving to a new area. More often than I care to admit, I have spooked bucks when I got up to leave, and they are normally good mature bucks.

To some hunters there is a great web of mystery surrounding horn rattling; however, there is nothing mysterious about it. You simply try to imitate the sounds of two bucks fighting.

Selecting Proper Rattling Sites

The best places to rattle in a buck are those areas where there is an abundance of bucks. Some authorities claim you can only rattle up bucks where the buck-to-doe ratio is no wider than one buck to three does. In truth you can rattle up whitetails nearly anywhere they exist, but only if the bucks are interested in responding. I have rattled up bucks in the Southeast where the deer were heavily hunted and the buck-to-doe ratio was as wide as one buck per 14 or 15 does. Just because the buck-to-doe ratio is wide does not mean you cannot rattle up a buck. However rattling works considerably better where there is a good or narrow buck-to-doe ratio. In such areas there are simply many more bucks than in places where there are fewer bucks—simple as that.

As to when to start rattling, generally bucks start responding to rattling horns as soon as they start actively making scrapes. This time varies greatly from one part of the South to another. In some parts of the South bucks can be rattled up in early October; in other parts it may be as late as the latter part of January. I have rattled up bucks as early as the last few days of September and as late as the last day of January.

Before discussing tactics, let me state that horn rattling can be exciting or totally frustrating. Some days bucks respond at every session, other days you cannot get a buck to respond for anything, or any way!

Rattling tactics should vary according to the status of the rut. Early in the fall when bucks are still roaming around together in bachelor herds, shortly after they have removed the velvet from their antlers, one of the best tactics is not rattling at all. Instead of rattling antlers, use your rattling horns to rub bushes and saplings.

During the early pre-rut, bucks spend considerable time rubbing their antlers to strengthen their neck muscles for future combat with other bucks. Deer are extremely curious and respond to the rubbing sounds to see what other bucks are in their area. I have "rubbed up" several bucks in southern Texas. One such buck was an eight point taken several years ago by my older daughter, Theresa. She shot the deer as it responded to her rubbing an antler, again on a small bush.

Another time, I had seen a buck on a couple of occasions near a remote waterhole before the season opened. When opening day arrived, I headed to the area intent on ambushing him as he came to water. I sat down on the tank dam where I had a commanding view of the area. About three in the afternoon I noticed the top of a bush shaking considerably more than the wind should cause it to sway. I suspected the cause of the shaking bush was a buck rubbing his antlers on it. I looked around and found a fairly stout stick and started rubbing a nearby mesquite tree (I had not brought my rattling horns with me). As soon as I started rubbing, the rubbing down behind the dam quit. I continued my rubbing for another minute or so, then slowly replaced the rubbing stick with my rifle. Less than three minutes later, the buck that had been rubbing his antlers appeared in an opening about 100 yards away. Through my variable scope cranked up to a full nine power I could see strips of bark

Theresa Weishuhn with a good eight point buck she "rubbed up" early in the fall.

hanging from around his antler bases. As the crosshairs moved back and settled on his shoulder I shot the 22 inch wide, long-tined eight point.

As the rut (peak of the breeding season) starts to approach, bucks start sparring, generally more pushing matches than serious fights, to test their mettle and their antlers. As two bucks begin to spar, they bring their antlers gingerly together, twist their heads back and forth, do some pushing, and then separate. Then they look around to see what other bucks might be watching. These sparring matches seldom last more than about 30 to 40 seconds. Sitting on food plots in the early fall I have seen as many as 15 to 20 bucks in the field at one time and have had five or six pairs of bucks sparring at the same time. It seems that one sparring match often causes other bucks to start sparring as well.

The last few days before the rut shifts into high gear, bucks start fighting in earnest. During this time they literally try to kill each other. There is nothing ritualistic about these types of fights; bucks are deadly serious! Fights may be brief or may last for hours. I have witnessed fights between two equally matched mature bucks that lasted for well over an hour, and some considerably longer. During this time they never once separated. The bucks would fight until they were practically exhausted. The two would lean into one another, breathe heavily, and rest. As soon as one regained some strength, the fight was on again. When two equally matched bucks fight, they make a tremendous amount of noise and racket and they push and shove each other over underbrush, fallen trees, rocks, and anything else that gets in their way. Bucks may also be vocal when they fight or right before, as they challenge each other. The vocalization may be a simple series of grunts, or even a snort-wheeze.

The snort-wheeze is not unlike a rapid "fit,fit,fit, fff-feeeeeeeeeeeeeeeeeee" sound. Of all the buck's vocalizations, this one indicates the greatest amount of intimidation and aggression. It is a buck's final warning before he intends to whip another buck. He may also make the sound after thoroughly thrashing another buck, and issuing a challenge to any and all comers.

When two big bucks fight they make a tremendous amount of noise. Quite frankly there is no way one human with a set of rattling horns can duplicate or even come close to duplicating all the noise made by two big bucks fighting, or by the other bucks that run in to see what bucks are fighting. However, this is the time to try to make as much noise as possible. Break limbs, roll rocks, grunt loudly, kick the ground with your heels–anything you can do to make as much noise as possible.

Rattling At Its Best

This is my favorite time to rattle. In South Texas this time generally occurs starting about the 15th of December. During this time it is not uncommon to rattle in 20 or more bucks in a single day on a well-managed ranch. While hunting the JDB Ranch near Cotulla in South Texas one December 19th, I rattled up 23 bucks between 4 and 5 o'clock in the afternoon. All but two of them were big mature bucks with eight or more points. I passed up numerous good 10 point bucks because they

132

Try to duplicate what bucks are doing during the various periods of the rut. Doing so will make you more successful.

appeared to need one more year before they would be prime or just past prime. I ended up shooting the twenty-third buck I rattled in. That one came in slowly, but at less than 10 yards from where I was seated near a big mesquite tree near a dense blackbrush thicket. I watched as the buck crossed a sendero, then moved around me to catch my scent. I shot the six-year-old, 19-inch-wide 11 point at less than eight paces. When rattling works, there is nothing that compares!

As the rut begins to wane, bucks still fight but they are seldom as serious or aggressive about fighting as they were only a couple of weeks earlier. Nor do they fight as long.

In rattling, try to duplicate what the deer are actually doing at the various phases of the rut. However, dare to be different. If bucks are not responding to the way you are rattling, try rattling a little longer, or do more rubbing on bushes.

The All Important Set-up

In setting up to rattle, do so where you can see any deer that responds. It does little good to rattle up a buck and not see him. I like to rattle close to thickets, or where I have previously seen bucks, and/or where there is an abundance of scrapes and rubs. If I am trying to rattle a buck out of a particular thicket, I will set up near the thicket but where the buck will have to cross some relatively open ground to see what is causing the rattling sounds. Such was the case with a buck I rattled up in the Southeast. I had found several fresh scrapes along the edge of a clear-cut that was starting to "heal over." About 30 steps into the cut-over area I picked out

Larry Weishuhn with a big 11 point buck he rattled up on the JDB Ranch in South Texas. It was the twenty-third buck he rattled up that December afternoon.

a low-growing shrub. The light wind was blowing from the shrub to the brush line. After the birds started chirping again, I started my rattling sequence. On my second series of rattling, the eight point poked his head out of the tree line and started coming my way. I waited until he had fully circled my position before taking the shot.

Some southern hunters swear by horn rattling, others swear at it! Some hunters successfully rattle up bucks from tree stands. I have done so on numerous occasions. However, I prefer to rattle from the ground. If I am hunting with a companion I will quite often put him up in a tree or stand where he can see a fair amount of countryside. Then I will stay on the ground and rattle for him or her. Throughout the day we alternate between being the horn rattler and the hunter. This technique has allowed me to take quite a few bucks.

The best time to rattle horns to attract bucks seems to vary from day to day. In some instances deer seem to respond best early in the mornings; in other instances, they may not respond at all until the middle part of the day. In reviewing my records as to when bucks respond best, I cannot see any obvious patterns relative to moon phases, temperature and winds (direction and velocity) or any other climatic conditions. One day the bucks may respond to nearly anything that remotely sounds like two bucks fighting. The next day, with all circumstances being the same as the day before, not a single buck will respond.

If you have not yet been successful at attracting bucks with rattling horns, do not give up. As I have mentioned horn rattling does not always work, and no one is going to be successful every time its tried. The other good thing about horn rattling is there is really no right or wrong way to rattle horns, regardless of what some hunters will tell you. When bucks want to respond, they will do so; if they don't, quite simply they won't. But once you have rattled in your first buck, to quote Anthony Ellis, a friend of mine from Tallapoosa, Georgia, you will be "plum rurrnt!"

Chapter 11

Hunting Natural Food Sources

Larry L. Weishuhn

Whitetails are ruminants that browse. Simply put, that means they have four chambers to their stomachs, including the rumen that serves as a storage area. This allows them to eat large quantities of rough forages and later chew their cud to continue the digestive process. Although they are selective, they eat a wide variety of leaves and twigs, fruits and mast crops, weeds and many other vegetative food items. What they eat depends upon where they live, the season of the year, and what is available at the time.

The key to finding whitetails in southern habitats is locating their current food supply. To do so, you have to know what they are eating in the area you are hunting at that particular time of the hunting season. Additionally, you have to learn how to identify those plants and know where to find them in your immediate area.

Keys To Learning What Deer Eat

Learning what deer eat during the fall hunting season is not always easy, but if you do your homework it is possible to learn about a deer's food habits. In most ecological areas prior scientific research has been conducted to determine the food habits of the local deer herds. State wildlife departments and state land grant universities are ideal places to start looking for such published information. Occasionally it is available from local county Agricultural Extension agents, Soil Conservation Service biologists, and even private biologists. Talking to longtime hunters in the particular area you plan to hunt is also a good way to learn about what deer prefer to eat during the fall. Learn from the older hunters in your group. Many of us who hunt whitetails in the South learned about fall deer food habits from our fathers, grandfathers, and those who hunted with them. They learned from others or by observing deer and logging information gained from past successes. Also try to attend local deer management and hunting clinics and seminars and learn all you can

Visiting with successful hunters is an excellent way to learn about available natural food items in the area, and about what deer are eating at the time.

about favorite natural deer food items. These are popular through the South and throughout the rest of the country. Another way to learn what the local deer are eating at the time you are hunting is to open up the rumen of a recent hunter-taken deer. The rumen is the largest part or chamber of the stomach. It is easily recognizable due to its size. In addition, the rumen's interior wall is covered with papillae or small finger-like structures. While you may not be able to exactly identify all that you find, you certainly will be able to determine what is most prevalent in the first part of the deer's stomach that serves as a storage area.

Whitetails like variety in their diet. They seldom eat too much of any one item. However, there are certain food items that they prefer over others. Deer have a pointed muzzle that allows them to reach into various vegetation or through a leaf-littered forest floor and select the tastiest and most nutritious morsels. In some respects deer are like us when we are presented with a huge "salad bar" at a restaurant. We go through the line picking out the items we prefer and like best. But if some of our favorite salad items are not there or are no longer available, we determine what we select based on what is present. Deer do much the same.

Changes With The Season

Throughout the year deer food items change from month to month and season to season. For the most part we, as hunters, are primarily concerned with what deer are eating during the time we are in the fall woods, but we should also take time to learn what deer subsist on throughout the rest of the year. Doing so will certainly make us much better hunters.

Most southern deer hunters, as elsewhere, know deer prefer acorns during the fall. Mast crops such as acorns are high in carbohydrates and energy, both needed to help deer survive the harsh times of winter. In areas where there are white oaks, their acorns are preferred over others. The white oak is a relatively widespread tree, but in many of the areas I hunt in the Southwest, there are no oaks, and at best, only a few other trees. I would be extremely hard pressed to find a white oak tree in the Brush Country of south Texas. The only places you would find oaks in this part of the country are in the extreme east, north, or in a nursery. The same is true for beech trees. Southern hunters know deer love beechnuts, but in some areas these trees do not exist or the nuts quickly disappear.

Several years ago I had a bow hunting camp on one of the ranches I managed. The vast majority of hunters I had in camp were from central Georgia. They arrived intent on hunting natural food sources. The area they previously hunted in their home state was loaded with many white oaks and a variety of other oaks. They knew their local vegetation and how to hunt the various natural food sources. They were excellent hunters, but when they came to the Texas Hill Country they were at a total loss as to what deer ate or how to identify what deer preferred at that particular time. I felt much the same way the first couple of times I

Acorns are one of the primary deer foods throughout the South.

hunted in Georgia, Alabama, or several of the other states in the Southeast.

However, if we have hunted a fair amount in the past, we do or should know some of the basics of deer food habits, and some things are relatively universal. Where persimmon trees exist, deer, as well as a wide variety of other wildlife, love the fruit of these trees. Throughout the South there are persimmon trees even though they may look quite a bit different. In the Southeast the fruit is orange when it is ripe; in the Southwest the fruit is nearly black. In other areas the fruit or tunas of prickly pear cactus may replace the fruit of the persimmon as a favorite during a different time of the year. The same is true for the fruit of the tasajilla cactus. This pencil-like cactus produces a small bright red fruit that is a much preferred food item for deer in the Southwest.

Seed pods from trees are favorites of deer throughout the South. In the Southeast deer will shift to eating honey locust pods as soon as they start falling. The pulp around these seeds is extremely sweet and palatable. In the Southwest, mesquite trees produce seed pods that are equally sweet and preferred by deer.

Previously I mentioned acorns. I suppose all species of oaks produce acorns. In many areas of the South it is fairly common to find as many as five to ten species of oaks on the same hunting property. Some years all the oaks might produce acorns. Other years only a portion of the oaks will produce, and in the "tough" years, there might not be any acorns. When there are quite a few acorns, deer will likely prefer those produced by some species over those of others. They will eat these preferred acorns first, then shift to others that are less desirable or palatable.

On one of my first hunting trips to Alabama, having done my homework to learn about what deer ate in the immediate area, I arrived asking where the largest stand of white oaks were on the property. The camp manager seemed impressed I knew enough about southern whitetails to want to hunt where there were white oaks. But then he replied there had been a horrible acorn crop and the white oaks in his area simply failed to produce. He suggested I hunt a stand of red oaks. According to him they had produced a banner crop. Red oaks were a tree I thought I was familiar with since we had quite a few red oak trees where I grew up in the gravel hills on the edge of the Gulf Coast prairie. I soon learned what he called a red oak and what I expected to be a red oak were two completely different trees. For this reason it is always a good idea to learn the local names of plants for the immediate area you are planning on hunting. It can prevent a lot of confusion.

There was a time that most of us who hunt in the South only hunted fairly close to home. These days it is not uncommon for us to travel to several states to hunt each year, in completely different kinds of habitat and vegetation types. Recently I hunted with several hunters from South Carolina in southern Texas. It was their first trip to the Brush Country. When they arrived the local countryside looked like a desert that would be totally devoid of white-tailed deer. They must have thought that no self-respecting whitetail would be caught dead in an area where there were no tall trees and dense underbrush. They soon learned differently

Larry Weishuhn inspects persimmons while hunting in Georgia.

when the hunt started. Even so, it took them several days to adapt to the totally different vegetation. I remembered my first trip to the Southeast for deer and recalled thinking much of the same!

Take the time to learn what the local preferred deer browse species are, how to identify them, and what deer shift to when their preferred browse species are no longer available. Several years ago I hunted in Alabama early in the hunting season. We hunted in oak trees that were loaded with acorns. When I came back to the same area several weeks later, the acorns had all fallen and for the most part had been eaten. By then the deer were shifting to honeysuckle. It would have done little good for me to hunt in the oaks, hoping to find deer feeding on a food supply that was no longer available.

Glass The Treetops

The early fall is a good time to scout natural food sources for deer. In hunting in Alabama, Georgia, and even Texas, I have often set up in a rather open bottom and used my binocular to glass the surrounding trees, not only to spot trees that are laden with acorns or other mast crops, but also to look for squirrel activity. Squirrels prefer many of the same mast crop items as do deer. Where you find a lot of squirrels, there you will likely also find a considerable number of deer. This holds true throughout the year.

Following deer trails is another good way to find out what deer are eating at various times. Generally, such trails lead from bedding areas to food sources, or vice versa. These trails provide ideal ambush points. In setting up along such trails I look for tracks that "come and go." To determine what times deer use these trails I will often "brush out" a section and then return every few hours to see during which time period the deer are using the trails. I know there are numerous electronic gadgets on the market these days that, when set up, will register the exact times deer are coming by. If you like using such items, that is great. They can be extremely helpful, especially in research. But when it comes to hunting, I much prefer depending upon more woodsmanship ways to determine such information. It may not always be as accurate, but I get greater satisfaction from doing it my way than by using electronic devices. This is simply a personal preference. I know we deer hunters are becoming as gadget minded as the bass fishermen, but I still prefer the old ways.

While hunting in the Southeast I found a trail that wound through an area covered with oak trees. Acorns were just starting to fall, but they were dropping in great abundance. The ground was littered with acorns. I imagined it would be difficult to select simply one area to hunt, other than setting up along one of the trails that led from a dense thicket to the oak tree-covered slope.

Doing some quick scouting I found a trail that was simply a mass of tracks and located a tree on the side of the trail in a little saddle where the slight easterly breeze blew my scent away from where the deer would be crossing. A few minutes later I had crawled my climber about

Harold Knight, of calling fame, with a big southern buck he took while hunting a natural food source.

20 feet off of the ground so the deer would not see my movement. The first deer started making their way to the oaks at 2:15 p.m., only a few minutes after I had crawled into the tree. The rest of the afternoon it was like a parade. I saw does, fawns, young bucks, and even some middle-aged bucks. Few minutes went by that I did not see deer. However, I intended to take a mature buck, or not shoot. Although there were some tempting young bucks that meandered by, I elected not to shoot.

For the next two days I hunted the stand from daylight to dark and saw a great variety of deer, including several decent young eight point bucks. But I had taken such a buck in the same general area the year before and was now looking for a bigger one. After three days of hunting from the same stand, I decided to hunt another area of the rather large property, owned by a timber company.

Acorn Games

The area I scouted the next morning also had a few oak trees, yet for some reason the mast crop was not as good, nor were the acorns really dropping in abundance. However I noticed there were a considerable number of deer tracks leading to the few oaks with acorns. Before leaving the area of abundant acorns, I filled several small plastic bags with them and stored them in my day pack.

The following morning I crawled into one of the oaks that was just starting to drop what few acorns it had. The tree provided a view of several other trees and a couple of persimmon trees that had a fair amount of fruit still on the tree. Competition among the deer for those acorns was substantial. Several times I saw does stand on their hind legs and flail at each other, fighting for acorns. There were also some serious visual threats, such as hard stares and ears pinched tightly against the neck. Normally does are dominant animals throughout the year, until bucks with hardened horns approach them. In most instances the does will then give way. However, that was not the case with one doe I watched that morning. When a young six point buck approached her area where she was eating acorns, she started out with a hard stare, then raised her head and pinched her ears close to her neck. The young buck continued coming closer to her area. When he got a little closer she stood on her hind legs and slapped and struck the young buck with her right forefoot, hitting him just below the eye. Before he could retreat, the doe hit him across the bridge of his nose with her other forefoot. To say she was protective of the food supply she thought belonged to her would be an understatement!

After she ate all the acorns in sight and moved off, the young buck came back to the tree, but all the while looking for the old doe that taught him some table manners. As he started to leave, I dropped a few acorns from my stand–those that I had picked up in the other area the day earlier. When they hit the ground he turned and came back. I dropped several more acorns and he walked almost directly under my perch in the tall oak. Had I been interested in the buck, he would have been mine. However, I had no interest in taking a young buck. I knew I would be hunting later where the bag limits on does would be fairly liberal and the family larder would be stocked with fresh venison taken from does, rather than young bucks. The acorn dropping "trick" had worked several times in the past. It was a technique I picked up from the late Ben Rogers Lee with whom I occasionally shared the speaker podium at various outdoor and hunting shows.

Before the day was over, I had spotted numerous young bucks and does that had come to where I had been dropping acorns. Thankfully my pack was filled with acorns. One of the bucks that came to the sound was a good one, the kind I was hoping to take. Several times he almost offered a shot, but he managed to always keep some underbrush, tree, or limb between me and him. He had eight long points, with good mass and a spread just beyond his ears. What set him apart from other bucks was the purling on his antlers and the darkness, with nearly ivory white tips. The rack was beautiful.

I tried everything I could think of to entice him out of the brush or offer a clear shot, including grunting, light rattling, and even throwing acorns in his direction. I even considered throwing acorns at him! Occasionally the buck would disappear, then 20 minutes to an hour later he would reappear. As legal shooting time ended, I still had not had a good shot at him.

I returned early the next morning. He did not show that day or the next. The following morning I had to leave for home. A couple of friends hunted him as well, but no one ever saw him again.

Food supplies change throughout the fall and the hunter has to adjust accordingly to how and where he hunts. One of my favored hunting spots in the South is Cross Creek Hollow, a private area located in Alabama. The property is owned by J. Wayne and Sherry Fears. I usually manage to slip away a day or two each hunting season to hunt the wooded slopes that surround the Hollow. I enjoy the camp, the people, and hunting the deer that live there as well. To date I have not taken a deer at Cross Creek Hollow and I never may. However, that does not detract from my desire to hunt there.

One year I could not arrange my hunting schedule to get to Alabama until late in that state's season. Despite what many might think, not all of Alabama has a late rut. By the time I got there the rut had long since passed, as had the white oak acorns, beechnut, persimmon, and other preferred fruits and mast crops. Deer were still relatively abundant, however seeing them was going to require different hunting areas and techniques.

Watch The Honeysuckle Patches

Doing some preliminary scouting Wayne and I found the deer were feeding primarily on honeysuckle, which on the property is mainly found in one area. Several trails led from thickets and hillsides to the slope where the majority of the honeysuckle is found.

That afternoon I set up a hastily built ground blind on an opposite slope where I could watch the honeysuckle patch. During the early after-

144

Larry Weishuhn with a young southern whitetail taken as it fed on honey locust pods.

noon I was entertained by the other wildlife in the area including a variety of birds, squirrels, and even a beaver or two. Occasionally I could hear wild turkeys scratching in the leaves on the ridge back behind me.

My stand was set up so the wind was in my face and the sun was at my back. Just before sundown the first deer appeared, walking along a trail leading to the honeysuckle. Three does walked single file, followed by two fawns and a yearling six point buck. I watched as they started foraging on the leaves and vines of the highly palatable plant, made even more so by Wayne having applied a considerable amount of fertilizer on the slope earlier in the year.

Before legal shooting light ended that afternoon, I saw several more does and fawns. Then after it was too dark to shoot, I watched a mature buck simply appear on the slope, as if he had risen out of the ground. In retrospect, he was probably bedded right in the dense stand of honeysuckle and had remained bedded there until he felt it safe for him to move. I watched him until it got simply too dark to see, even through my binocular.

Early the next morning I was back, well before daylight. When the light finally turned a soft gray, I spotted a buck feeding on the honeysuckle. During the night a cold front had blown through and the skies were dark and dreary, threatening rain. In the poor light I could tell the deer was a buck, but little else. Finally he moved to a background where I could see his rack–a fairly tall eight point. I waited to raise my rifle, wanting to determine through my binocular whether or not he was the buck I had seen the afternoon before. I scanned the honeysuckle-covered ridge and spotted several more deer, either feeding or moving to the slope to feed.

Finally it got light enough to clearly see the buck. A quick glance told me the buck was likely a two-year-old buck and he obviously needed at least one or two more falls to attain the type of antlers and age I was interested in taking.

The rest of the trip I saw several other bucks and numerous does and fawns, but never a buck I wanted to take. Nonetheless I took great pleasure in the hunt. I had seen numerous deer, including several bucks that I could have easily taken, had I wanted to do so. I was also pleased at having determined what the deer were eating and then hunting those areas. The bucks that were passed would be in the same general area in the future and there was always the next trip to the Hollow to look forward to!

Hunting natural food sources requires doing your homework and a fair amount of legwork to determine where the favored deer food sources are on the property you hunt. You may also have to learn to adjust, much like the deer that live in your hunting area. But if you do things right and shoot straight, the rewards are well worth the effort.

Chapter 12

Stand Placements, Another Term For Ambushing

Bill Bynum

Tree stands and where they are placed are vital elements to hunting success. It is simply a fact that before a hunter can harvest a deer, a deer must be present. This is the reason hunters spend countless hours scouting the hunting area to make a determination of where they will encounter their game, and to find the exact position that will make the deer available to them! In short, we scout to find the perfect ambush point. But what is the perfect ambush point? In my opinion, it should contain three important factors.

Naturally, the first factor is that the area must provide the hunter with game. Without the presence of game, there will be nothing to ambush. The second factor is that the area should not defy the full potential of the hunter. An ambush point should allow a hunter to maximize his or her capabilities. If a bow hunter is capable of properly executing a 30-yard shot, the area should provide for this. The same goes for a gun hunter. In short, the more area a hunter can utilize, the better the odds for success. The third factor is the ambush area should allow the hunter to remain as the hunter, and not the hunted! Many times we fail to realize certain factors that reverse the role we intend to portray.

Experienced hunters know the slightest noise or movement can foil the best hunting plans. This is why it is important to consider various elements of proper ambush points.

One of the key factors in learning to properly ambush deer is concealment. Concealment from the keen eyes of our game is vital to successful hunting. Hunters should remember white-tailed deer can detect the slightest movement. This is why it is important for the hunter to be concealed to some degree, in order to simply reduce the odds of deer detecting the hunter's presence. This is also the reason we should distort our human outline while hunting.

Portable stands and their placement have become important to modern day hunting. (Photo credit: J. Wayne Fears)

A Lesson Learned The Hard Way

The early days of my hunting career were often days of frustration. I often felt the world was passing me by while I sat upon a wooden board. The board straddled two limbs in a red oak tree. From this position, I could spy on a big cornfield in which I had seen numerous bucks. It would be from this makeshift blind that I would shoot the buck of my dreams. This played over and over in my youthful mind. Days turned into weeks with me spending every available minute on the board. Many times I would see deer at the end of the field. The distance between the deer and me was beyond the range of my shotgun slug. Though this was frustrating, the thought of the deer avoiding me was a greater frustration. I simply could not understand why the deer would not come closer. The deer would begin browsing towards me and suddenly stop. Upon stopping, the animals would stare in my direction for long periods of time, then reverse their movements.

Finally I decided something was wrong and it was time to find out what. The following afternoon found me on the side of the cornfield nestled in some honeysuckle bushes. The sun was slowly sinking when I spotted movement in the woods bordering the field. From 50 yards away the white-throated patch of the doe was clear. In seconds two other does joined her, standing just inside the timber. Several minutes passed as the deer stared in the direction of my tree stand. This was somewhat surprising to me as I realized the animals were looking at the stand. Soon they entered the field for their daily feeding. At one point the deer were less than 20 yards away from me. Sitting completely still, I watched the movements of the does closely. It was again surprising to see the deer closely watching my old stand. It was at this point in time I realized I could easily see the board. I also realized that if I had been in the stand, my outline would have been apparent. I then began to wonder how many bucks had stood inside the woods and watched me sitting on that old board. Today, I still wonder how many of those trophy bucks watch me as I sit in proper concealment!

Often I think hunters make the mistake of concealing themselves too much. I have seen hunters who place so much brush around the stand or blind that they could not see out of it. Though this may sound funny, it is a fact! Visibility is an important factor in successful hunting. The more visibility a hunter has, the earlier the game can be detected. This, in turn, permits the hunter to decide and prepare for the shot.

When preparing a stand or blind, only enough brush is needed to distort the human outline, nothing more. The brush or distorting material should be placed so it will not come in contact with the hunter's movement. This not only allows freedom of movement, but reduces the noise factor.

The Noise Factor

Every hunting season hundreds of deer are saved by hunter-related noise. Many of these sounds are created by the stands or blinds from which we hunt. In my opinion, hunting stands are possibly the most

Never take for granted the eyes of white-tailed deer, or their intelligence level either!

overlooked piece of equipment used. For some reason, many hunters simply fail to check their stands for noise prior to hunting.

Before the days of portable tree stands I hunted from homemade ladder stands. These were constructed from boards and planks nailed together. Most ladder stands supported a platform of plywood for standing on while hunting. These stands also proved to be great muscle builders by the time they were carried to the hunting site. The stand would be attached to the tree with a length of rope or chain. At that time we felt these twelve-foot high marvels were the ultimate in deer hunting. Well, maybe they weren't the ultimate in hunting, but they were in teaching. This taught me what and what not to do from a ladder stand.

It also quickly taught me the benefits of safety belts. Most of the time the safety belt was a piece of rope left over from the stand construction, but it kept me from taking a 12-foot plunge on numerous occasions, and that's what counted. The ol' ladder stand also taught me the importance of distorting my human outline, as previously discussed. It also taught me to respect the hearing of the white-tailed deer even more than I had.

The lesson began one afternoon while I was bow hunting. I had been in the old ladder stand for hours. Darkness was quickly descending upon the woods when I heard the snapping of a twig. Instantly I looked in the direction of the noise. To my surprise, I discovered a handsome buck coming towards me. In only minutes the deer was standing broadside to me. I knew the arrow would travel less than 15 yards before connecting with the buck. The buck would soon be mine. I could feel it!

Wooden ladder stands or portable stands can create noises–noises that can cost you the buck of a lifetime!

Slowly I began drawing my bow as the deer presented the perfect shot. With only a slight shift of my feet, I would be in perfect shooting position. I had barely moved my foot forward when disaster occurred. The shifting of my body weight on the wooden frame produced a low volume "cr-ee-eee-k" beneath me. Though the noise seemed low in volume to my ears, it was not low in volume to the deer. With the sound of the ladder stand, the buck quickly turned its head towards me. Now I had lost the element of surprise as the buck was fully alerted. The tension within me quickly transformed to panic as the buck stared at me.

Standing with the bow fully drawn, I could feel my muscles tighten. Knowing I could not hold the power of the bow much longer, I released the arrow. The bright yellow fletch of the arrow instantly marked where the buck stood. In the time it takes to blink your eye the buck had escaped me. Many hours of hard work and preparation had now been wasted because I had not thoroughly prepared my stand. I had neglected to inspect the stand for noise.

Since that day I have learned cooking oil can be helpful in producing deer steaks. By taking regular cooking oil and saturating areas where stand noises occur, the problem can be corrected. I recommend applying the oil weeks prior to hunting season to permit the scent to dissipate. This is important as corn oil is not a natural scent of the woods.

I can still recall the first portable climbing stand I ever saw. I met a hunter on some public hunting land with one of these contraptions on his back. After a few minutes of inquiring about the stand, I knew I had to have one. For a number of years that old Baker brand climbing stand served me well. Today, however, portable tree stands are much lighter and safer. Portable tree stands have just about become a must for the serious deer hunter.

Sadly, many hunters fail to realize that, even with the modern tree stand, preparation must be made. Modern tree stands can and will produce noise. This is especially true when materials such as aluminum or plastic are being used. Unfortunately, corn oil has little effect on these materials.

To eliminate noise from a modern tree stand I recommend the following: First, place rubber washers against all bolts and nuts of the stand. Bolts and nuts are generally used to connect different parts of the stand to form the stand. Then place a heavy amount of unscented petroleum jelly around the rubber washers. This will serve as a form of lubrication for the parts. The next step is to place pieces of thin rubber on areas where the materials may be touching. I have found the use of a bicycle tire repair kit to be excellent for this. The small rubber patches eliminate the sounds of metal touching metal.

Another step in preparing my portable tree stand is platform preparation. Today some tree stands are factory-equipped with felt or carpet on the standing platform. If mine is not, I will self-install some outdoor carpet on the platform.

The final step I take in preparing my tree stand is to eliminate the "pingers." Pingers are areas on the stand that could produce a noise if touched by a bow or gun. Areas such as guardrails or handles can pro-

Many hunters fail to realize the noises created by portable tree stands.

duce an alarming sound. This is the reason I cover such areas with foam rubber and heavy cloth. The foam rubber serves as a cushion upon contact. The cloth also serves as a buffer and scent dispenser.

Stinking Stands

Scent has become a highly debated subject among hunters. Many feel the use of commercial cover scents is a waste of money. These hunters believe a deer is going to smell you no matter what is applied. To this I say, "More power to you, but give me my cover scent!" I am a firm believer in the use of cover scents. This is especially true when I am hunting with archery equipment. The reason is simple. I must have the deer in close range before I can attempt a shot. Cover scents permit or aid in accomplishing this objective.

The manner in which I use cover scents may vary from the standard practices of some hunters. Most hunters using cover scents place the scents on themselves and nothing else. I place cover scent on anything that could produce an alarming odor to the deer. This includes my bow and my tree stand.

Unlike some hunters, I prefer to leave little to chance. I like to have all the possible odds in my favor. This is the reason I prepare my tree stand and its location for scent. Preparation of the tree stand begins weeks before the actual hunt. In doing so, I wash the stand thoroughly with a non-scented detergent and water. After the washing is completed, I rinse the stand thoroughly with a garden hose to remove all remaining dirt. Then I allow the stand to dry in an open area, free of pets or children.

A week prior to hunting I will then take the tree stand to my chosen hunting site. I check the stand for noise and prepare the tree for the stand. I also prepare the area for my cover scent. This preparation is done with the help of a discarded piece of cloth. I place the cloth approximately one foot above my designated stand elevation. Next I apply a generous amount of the selected cover scent to the cloth and leave the area. This preparation allows the cover scent to remain within the given area. This then allows the deer to become accustomed to the cover scent. In summary, it is like the smell of a new car until the first payment is due!

Many hunters view tree stand positioning like gambling. They close their eyes, point their right index finger, spin around three times, and stop. The closest tree the finger is pointing at receives the tree stand. If you were born under a lucky star, this method might work. If you are like me, the tree would break in half beneath your elevated stand. Though this might sound humorous, it is a serious matter.

Selecting a tree in which to place your tree stand should be taken seriously–in fact, as seriously as protecting your life! This is because you could well be doing just that! You should always select *live* trees. *Never* place a your tree stand in a dead or decaying tree. Dead or decaying trees could easily break from the pressure of a hunter's weight. Always inspect for decaying limbs that could fall on you. Experience has taught

Never place a tree stand in or around a decaying tree.

me it is always wise to inspect the trees nearby. The length of a crashing tree can go a long way, and you don't want to be in its path!

When selecting a tree in which to position a tree stand, some important factors should be considered. One such factor is shooting distance. Bow hunters are influenced by this more than gun hunters. Bow hunters must be able to have the game within the limitations of their equipment. Most bow hunters prefer to have the shooting distance under 30 yards. Remaining within 30 yards allows hunters to maximize the potential of today's standard hunting equipment. Therefore, the more target areas (trails, scrapes, feeding areas, etc.) within the range, the better the odds for success. This is why the tree stand should be located in, or near, the center of the target zone. By positioning the stand in the center, hunters can utilize more of the area than positioning it on the edge of the area.

How High Is High Enough

Another factor in tree stand positioning is elevation. I have listened to some pretty heated debates over tree stand elevation. In most cases these debates were among bow hunters. These hunters debated what was the proper elevation from which to hunt. Some hunters said the higher, the better. These hunters believed the higher the stand position, the lower the odds of being detected by the deer. A valid point, I agree.

The other side argued the factor of the shooting angle. These hunters stressed the importance of obtaining the best possible shot angle for maximum penetration within the target. In many instances, the shooting angle is decreased with each degree of elevation. Another valid point. So who really is correct? Both are, in my opinion. The proper elevation of a tree stand is a decision only the individual hunter can make. I think both factors must be taken into consideration when placing the tree stand. Most hunters will have a good idea of the target that will present itself. It is with this knowledge both principles should be applied. I do, however, place more emphasis on shot angle than on elevation.

During my lifetime, I have had the privilege of hunting with some fine hunters. I have also hunted with some highly amusing chaps! From the experiences with the latter, I have learned many things of *what not to do* in the woods. One such thing is not to use the sun as part of my hunting strategy. This lesson was administered to me by a high school friend. My friend would go to great lengths to ensure the sun would be directly behind him while hunting. He believed by doing this, the deer would be blinded if they should look up at him. True, there may be some merit to this principle, but in my opinion, little merit. In fact, I believe the animals

The angle of the shot is important, especially for the bow hunter.

Old abandoned stands can be useful, even when they are not being used!

would see him before they became blinded by the sun. However, I do prefer the sun to be casting its rays from either left or right of my position. I have often detected deer in front of me from the sun's reflection on them.

Detouring For Deer

During recent years I have read countless words pertaining to tree stand positioning. Like most of you, I have often questioned the author's judgment concerning the subject matter. This is especially true when I read that crossing the primary target area will not affect the animals. To me, this is like saying someone has hidden three dozen land mines in my yard and I have nothing to worry about!

When crossing the primary hunting area on the way to our stand position, we are disturbing the area. The degree of disturbance will vary according to the area, the existing conditions, and the hunter. Therefore, I feel no matter how cautious we are, we still leave some evidence of our travel. True, maybe all the deer are not affected by this, but who really knows? This is the reason I will divert from crossing the area whenever possible. If this means I have to walk a little more to the stand, I will do it. In short, the sneakier we are, the better.

Today my wooden ladder stands of years gone by stand as mementos of the many incidents that occurred from their platforms. They are reference points for many successful hunts, and for the countless failures. Luckily, many of the failures influenced the success stories. In summary, I learned a lot from the old wooden tree stands.

Today, the majority of the wooden stands are beyond supporting a hunter safely. Like skeletons of the past, the stands are a lonely sight. Some would ask why do I not remove them if they are not being used? The reason is that I still use them! I have used these old stands to divert deer from one area into another–from the area of the old stand site into my primary hunting area. How?

Many of the old wooden stands remain on active deer trails. Like most deer trails, they lead from feeding to bedding areas, or vice versa. Some trails are more active than others. Naturally, I will hunt from the most active trail, but if an old stand is on a secondary trail, or another nearby trail, I activate the old stand. To activate the stand, I will place the sight and smell of a human on the old stand. This is accomplished by placing a few small pieces of tissue paper so they flow freely in the breeze. The scent is created by placing a cheap bottle of dime store cologne at the base of the old stand.

I have no way of knowing the exact number of deer I have diverted over the years, but I do know the handsome nine pointer on my office wall shunned the smell of Old Spice!

Chapter 13

Open Country Bucks

Larry L. Weishuhn

Mention hunting white-tailed deer in the South and most hunters conjure up thoughts of dense deer woods comprised of hardwood and pine, rolling hills covered with tall trees, dense thickets of briars and brambles, oaks and Spanish moss and swamps. While these are great and somewhat typical places to hunt, they are certainly not the only places to hunt southern whitetail. While I have hunted deer in many of the southern states, I will be the first to admit I am somewhat biased. My favorite place to hunt deer is in my home state of Texas.

Open country whitetails are often overlooked.

Normally a hunter's first time visit to Texas is met with doubts that the desert-like terrain will support much more than long-eared jackrabbits, coyotes and rattlesnakes. Admittedly we do have our share of those critters, but we also have a great white-tailed deer herd—one of the finest in North America. Some hunters think the only place to hunt for big whitetails in Texas is the famed Brush Country. True, it is a great area to hunt and it produces some truly outstanding deer. In the following chapter I will discuss hunting the brushy habitat of southern Texas. But some of the more interesting whitetail hunting takes place in the relatively open areas of northern Texas and the wide open sandy plains on the eastern edge of southern Texas.

Hunting Whitetails Where The Buffalo Roamed

One of my favorite areas to hunt whitetails in North America is in the northern part of Texas, which lies basically north and west of a line from San Angelo to Abilene to Fort Worth. The country consists of flat plains, small table-top mesas, relatively open country with only a scattering of brush. For the most part it looks much more like pronghorn antelope habitat than whitetail habitat, but do not be fooled. The relatively open country produces some extremely big bucks, often characterized by long brow tines.

Ranches in the area are large, even by Texas standards. For the most part these are large cattle ranches, where owners and managers take great pride in their wildlife and especially their whitetails and wild turkeys. Many of the ranches are leased on a long-term basis to hunters. But there are also numerous ranches that offer package-type hunts (three- to five-day, fully outfitted and guided hunts).

The primary food sources for whitetail that live here are forbs. Thus the deer herd is highly dependent upon rainfall. If there is sufficient rainfall, then the deer will thrive. If there is little precipitation, then deer may well suffer. When the area has three or four back-to-back years of relatively wet weather, there is no finer whitetail hunting in North America.

In this area it is not uncommon to find deer roaming in herds, such as you would expect of prairie animals. One year while I was conducting a game survey on a large ranch west of San Angelo in early September, I counted 73 bucks in one large bachelor herd. All but two had eight or more points. Never before or since have I seen that number of bucks staying together in a single herd. I saw the same herd of bucks about a week later and it still contained 52 bucks—all had impressive racks. During the same survey I often spotted herds of 20 or more deer. While such large herds are not that common, they do exist. More commonly I have seen herds of 5 to 20 animals.

Hunting in relatively open whitetail habitat takes a lot of glassing of the areas having potential for deer. One of the masters at glassing for open country whitetails and then stalking to within easy rifle range is Greg Simons, a wildlife biologist/hunting outfitter who operates Wildlife Sys-

160

tems, Inc., headquartered in San Angelo, Texas. I have often hunted white-tails with Greg.

On one of those hunts we crawled to the top of a mesa well before day-light. The first light was gray, but it soon turned rosy, illuminating the tall prairie grasses and the long tines of a bedded buck. I had glassed the shal-low draw where the buck was bedded only moments before and did not see the antler tips. Greg had to point the buck out to me.

All that was visible of the buck were the tips of his antlers. But what I saw was of great interest. It looked as if the buck had 12 typical points with about a 20-inch outside spread. No doubt I was interested. One of my whitetail hunting goals was and remains to take a typical 12 point buck. With that statement you likely have guessed I did not get the buck, but it was no one's fault but my own.

As soon as we spotted the buck, we glassed the surrounding area and found we could probably get within about 300 yards of the animal. By dropping off of the backside of the mesa and then crawling across several draws, taking advantage of what little cover there was, there was a good chance I would finally take that typical 12 point. Several times during the stalk we crawled right up to bedded does and smaller bucks, only to have to retreat and start again on a different route. Thankfully the weather was relatively cool and snakes were already in their dens.

After about an hour we finally topped the small rise that would allow us to see the bedded buck. Ever so slowly we peeked over the edge. Through my binocular I could clearly see the buck's rack and about eight inches of his neck. The buck was facing down the slope, watching the valley below. Both Greg and I guessed the distance at 300 yards, a long way, but not an impossible distance from which to make a killing shot. Prior to going on the hunt I had spent considerable time at the range shooting my .280 Rem-ington at that distance, both from the bench and from other shooting posi-tions.

Had the grass not been tall, I would likely have had a Harris Bipod, but I knew the tall grass would prevent taking a shot from such a low level. For that reason I had picked up a couple of sotol (a dagger-like plant typical of the Southwest) stalks to use as a crossed sticks rest.

Greg and I watched the buck for several minutes. During this time I tried to control my breathing and settle down. While I have taken a fair number of good bucks in the past, I get overly excited at the possibility of taking a good buck. The opportunity at a typical 12 point must have caused my adrenaline level to increase dramatically. Slowing down my heart rate and excited breathing was no easy chore.

Finally I started settling down and rested the .280 Remington on the crossed sticks. The crosshairs of the Simmons variable, cranked up to 10 power, weaved back and forth across the deer's neck. I decided not to shoot and simply wait until the deer decided to stand up, no matter how long it took.

While we waited, we glassed the lower country below us. In so doing we spotted four more bucks, all eight to 10 points. They, too, were bedded. We also saw several does, in groups of 4 to 12. Some of the does were bed-ded, while others fed on low-growing forbs. As the sun came across a distant mesa and shone on "my" bedded 12 point, I hoped he would stand to stretch or start to feed.

I had my binocular trained on the bedded buck when he stood, but before I could trade them for the rifle, the buck took off running. He disappeared over the edge of the small rise where he had been bedded. Just that quick, he was gone. Try as Greg and I might, we could not locate the buck again. Where he went, we do not know.

On other hunts with Greg I have been more successful in taking the bucks we hunted, as have many other hunters. For that reason when *Deer & Deer Hunting* magazine chose an outfitter to use for a special sweepstakes hunt in 1994, they chose Greg's Wildlife Systems. The sweepstakes winner/hunter was Dan Ruben of Wisconsin. Dan's first look at the open country whitetail habitat made him wonder what he had gotten into. The countryside was not anything like his normally wooded deer hunting area back home. But after the first morning's hunt with guide Brown Delozier, he was convinced there certainly were deer in the open country. With the hunt quickly coming to an end and after passing up many white-tailed bucks each day, he took a beautiful eight point that was feeding out of a patch of tall grass.

The Case Of The Disappearing Deer

Hunting on the spacious Nail Ranch just north of Albany I have seen bucks simply disappear into a sea of tall prairie grass. One of the best

Dan Ruben with a good buck he took while hunting the open country of north Texas with Greg Simons' Wildlife Systems, Inc., of San Angelo, Texas.

bucks I have seen on that ranch was of near record book quality. We jumped him from a grassy draw as we were driving back to camp during the middle of the day. He took off running, going across a broad tall-grass plain. Suddenly he simply dove into the grass. We hurried to the exact spot where he disappeared. For the next 30 minutes we walked back and forth in the area, trying to find or jump him again in hopes of getting a shot. He was not to be found. What he did after he dove into the grass, I have no way of knowing. He simply disappeared and was not seen again. When he disappeared into the grass it was as if he was diving into a pool of water. That was it!

I have seen the same thing happen several other times. On another hunt on the Nail, this one on horseback, Craig Winters and I spotted a buck on a distant hillside. The buck was feeding and was surrounded by three does. He made a rush at them. When they paid him little attention he walked to a clump of bluestem grass and laid down. Immediately Craig and I started our stalk. We were never out of sight of where the buck had bedded. When we could not spot the bedded buck, we decided to walk in and try to jump him.

We walked exactly to where we had watched the buck bed. He was nowhere to be seen. We walked all through the area and never again saw the buck. I have simply come to expect that sort of thing from open country bucks.

As to what happens to the bucks such as those I mentioned, the only explanation I have is that they simply crawl away. One day while hunting with Johnnie Hudman on the Nail, he and I were sitting on a ridge over-looking a huge tall grass plain below us. In the distance we saw a couple of hunters. They soon spotted a buck Johnnie and I were watching a long way below us. The two began their stalk and apparently disappeared from view of the buck when they got to within about 300 yards. As soon as the bedded buck saw them disappear, he literally crawled from one thick patch of grass to another until he could slip into a thick grass-covered draw. Once there, he kept his head down and his tail tucked until he was below and behind them. Perhaps the bucks I had seen and then "lost" had done much the same.

The open country of north Texas also gave me the opportunity to take a monstrous buck whose shed antlers we had found the previous year, after a controlled burn to stimulate grass and weed growth. The only woody vegetation in the area were several old mesquite trees. The morning I had the opportunity at the buck, we jumped him as we were walking to an area where we intended to rattle. The moment I saw him I knew it was him. Quickly I brought my rifle to my shoulder and concentrated on making a killing shot. When the crosshairs settled on a vital area, I squeezed off. The buck kept running and disappeared into a thick grass draw and was gone. Behind me I could hear my companion, Dan Walker, laughing. My having just missed the deer might have been somewhat humorous to him, but I could not see any reason for his laughing to the point of rolling on the ground and hooting. I was about to get perturbed when my compadre started pointing at a mesquite limb only about five

Baseball great Nolan Ryan with a buck he shot, after Larry Weishuhn missed it by centering a mesquite limb.

feet in front of where I stood. There in the center of the limb was a small hole, made by a 7mm bullet.

That afternoon, baseball great Nolan Ryan, hunting in the same area where I missed the buck, took the same deer. He narrowly missed the Boone and Crockett record book. Thankfully not all of my open country whitetail hunts have ended in the same way.

The eastern part of South Texas is a sandy land of wide open spaces, tall grass and weeds, occasional mottes of mesquite and other thorn bushes, and some extremely big white-tailed deer. This area is where many of the first Spanish settlers established the ranching tradition that exists in Texas today. The area was once home to huge herds of wild horses—so many that it was given the name "The Wild Horse Desert." The wild horses may be gone, but the descendants of the whitetails that roamed the open sand country remain today. Hunting there can truly be an adventure, where you never know how large the next buck might be as it appears out of the tall grass.

Hunting The Wild Horse Desert

For the past several years it has been my pleasure to work with numerous ranches in the area as a consulting biologist, and to hunt large ranches such as the Encinitos. The Encinitos has been in the same family for many years; hopefully, it will be that way for many more years.

Hunting this type of open country is not particularly easy. Often it requires quietly still-hunting from one small motte of brush to another and spending considerable time glassing. These mottes are often separated from one another by several hundred yards of grassy plains. Deer are likely to show up anywhere, especially during the breeding season, when most hunters hunt the area.

As the rut approaches, one day the open country is nothing but a sea of grass, the next day bucks seem to be moving everywhere you look. On a good day I have seen as many as 20 to 25 "shooter" bucks. On another day hunting there I might only see one buck and few other deer.

Bill Whitfield glasses the open country of South Texas, home to some extremely good bucks and whitetail hunting.

The most common way of hunting the open country of south Texas is for hunters to cruise ranch roads looking for deer. In Texas it is legal to hunt from vehicles as long as you are hunting on private property. While this is a "social" way of hunting, it is only successful on big bucks right during the heat of the rut. Even then the bigger mature bucks have long since learned to avoid vehicles, or at least most of them.

One hunting season Encinitos' hunt outfitter, Bill Whitfield of San Antonio, Texas, and I were driving the eight miles from the hunting camp to the front gate to put up a sign for a film crew that was coming down to videotape a hunt. On the way to the front gate we found a monstrous typical 11 point with one kicker on his typical five side. He was with a doe and totally oblivious to our presence. I stared at the buck through the Simmons scope mounted on my .309 JDJ Contender handgun. The buck was less than 50 yards away and I could have easily taken him. But I passed. Why?

When Bill and I had driven to the camp several of the commercial hunters were sitting around the large dinner table lamenting and complaining that they were not seeing any deer. I commented that Bill and I had seen several good bucks on the way into camp, and that likely due to the full moon the bigger bucks were moving during the middle of the day. None of the hunters were ever going to be able to take a good deer sitting at the table talking about a lack of deer on the ranch. Thus, when Bill and I saw the near record book buck, we decided it would be a good idea to pass. It would not be appropriate for the ranch biologist to be on the ranch less than 20 minutes and take a huge buck, especially when the other hunters in camp still had not taken their deer. I have also long believed that my game management work on a ranch precluded me from hunting and taking the best bucks available on those ranches. I believe such opportunities belong to the paying hunters. That unfortunately being the case, I passed on the buck.

When we got back to camp three of the four hunters had taken good mature bucks. For the rest of the hunting season Bill and his hunters looked for the big buck I passed up. He was not seen again that fall. The following year he was taken by former baseball player Greg Olson, under somewhat similar circumstances as when I saw the deer. Greg, along with his guide and a cameraman, were headed back to camp for lunch when they spotted the buck at a great distance. Hurriedly they parked their vehicle and proceeded stalking the deer. Twenty minutes later they had cut the distance to about 250 yards. Due to the open country there was no way to get any closer. Greg took careful aim and moments later claimed his near record book buck. As in many areas throughout the South and the rest of North America, big bucks often move during the middle of the day.

While on a scouting trip to the open, sandy country of southern Texas, I spotted a mature buck with 10 basic points and split back tines. He would make an ideal buck to hunt. He had a good rack and was mature. Taking him would be a challenge! Even though guide John Pfluger saw him a couple of times before the hunting season, there was no guarantee we would be able to find him when I got down to the Encinitos to hunt.

Larry Weishuhn with a good buck taken on the Encinitos Ranch in the Wild Horse Desert area of Texas. This buck was rattled up by John Pfluger.

There has been much written about patterning bucks. Some can be patterned and some cannot. I have learned if you spend too much time trying to pattern a buck, you simply cause him to change his ways. The same time you are trying to pattern a buck, he is patterning you!

John spent some time watching for the buck from a vantage point, a tall stabilized sand dune. During his scouting trips he spotted the buck only one time. When I got to the Encinitos we decided to hunt from a couple of tripods, positioned next to a mesquite near the spot where the buck had been seen earlier.

The sun had not yet risen from its grassy bed when John started rattling. Off in the distance, nearly as far away as I could see, there he came at a trot, the buck we were looking for. Occasionally all that was visible of him were his antlers appearing to float over the top of the tall grass. There was little doubt he was coming directly to the antlers. I waited until the buck stopped less than 50 yards away before squeezing the trigger.

Hunting open country takes a lot of patience, whether you spend hours glassing and then stalking or still-hunting moving slowly through the tall grass from one small rise to another. It is unlike hunting any other southern white-tailed deer habitat!

Chapter 14

Brush Country Bucks

Larry L. Weishuhn

The Brush Country of South Texas is a land where nearly everything has thorns and spines. It is an arid, desert country comprised of large privately owned ranches where landowners are interested not only in cattle ranching, but also in wildlife and especially the quality white-tailed deer that live there. This area has long been famous for big white-tailed bucks and lots of them. Few if any other hunting places can compare. Much of the interest we currently see in quality deer throughout North America can be attributed to what was started in South Texas. It was here that quality deer management techniques now being used across the continent were developed and perfected.

Noticing the quality of the local South Texas deer herd was slipping back in the early 1970s, biologists such as Al Brothers and Murphy Ray and a few others started working with landowners and hunters to halt the decline. We began talking about and then promoting proper harvest of both sexes, as well as improving the habitat. Thus, the quality deer management movement was born. The movement has since spread throughout much of the South, as well as other parts of the country.

Where Quality Deer Management Was Born

Quality white-tailed deer management was born in South Texas, and it is there that it is most practiced. The result is some of the finest white-tailed deer hunting to be found anywhere in North America.

When those who hunt whitetails are asked where they would choose to hunt if given the chance, a preponderance of hunters reply "South Texas!" Few places have a better reputation for producing big-racked whitetails than does the Brush Country.

I first became involved with quality deer management programs in South Texas around 1970. During those early years I did my share of shooting does throughout Texas and especially on ranches in the southern part of the state while working on various nutrition research. In those early years, quite often those were the only does shot in South

Beth Weishuhn with a good whitetail taken in the Brush Country.

Texas. Hunters initially were reluctant to harvest any does, as were land-owner/managers. It seemed to take forever, but eventually the idea of taking does started taking hold, as did the ideas of passing up young bucks, conducting proper livestock grazing techniques, and even improving habitats. Along the way those ranchers and hunters who got involved in quality deer management programs started seeing the benefits of their efforts. Soon others saw the results achieved by their neighbors and friends and they, too, became involved in similar programs. The idea of being able to produce a quality deer herd started snowballing. Deer and hunting in South Texas have improved ever since, as well as throughout North America.

Hunting Where Big Bucks Abound

Hunting in the Brush Country is a pure pleasure. I have hunted whitetails throughout North America and nowhere have I seen as many or better whitetails than on well-managed South Texas ranches. Quite often I have hunted on ranches where it was not uncommon to see 20 or more bucks per day. During one particular hunt on a ranch just a few miles south of where I live, I shot the 121st buck, eight point and better, I saw during a three-day hunt. Other hunters in this area have experienced the same.

One year while working on a video and television production with The Nashville Network's "Realtree Outdoors," we hunted on the Perlitz Ranch near Crystal City. The ranch is one that has been under a quality deer management program for numerous years. The rut was just about to begin. It was a time when deer were really moving well. Sitting in a blind overlooking a feeding area, my cameraman and I had as many as 26 bucks in sight at one time; all had eight or more points. Others on the ranch saw as many and more each time they hunted, morning or afternoon.

Hunting on the JDB Ranch near Cotulla during mid-December, in less than an hour I rattled up 23 eight-point-and-better bucks. On a ranch in Webb County just north of Laredo where I frequently hunted in the past, on numerous occasions I saw as many as 20 or more bucks in a day. Many others who have hunted South Texas have experienced the same, or saw even more bucks in a day.

I do not mean to imply every hunting day in South Texas is going to be like what I just described. Some seasons I have hunted for several days before seeing my first mature buck. Big mature bucks are never easy, no matter where you hunt. However, I have hunted whitetails throughout North America and have never seen deer hunting that equals hunting in the Brush Country of South Texas.

Most who have hunted the region will agree there is a special mystique about hunting this arid region. You never know what kind of buck will step out of the mesquite and cactus when you hunt the Brush Country. The area just south of the Rio Grande in Mexico is much the same.

This region may offer some of the finest whitetail hunting anywhere, but virtually all the whitetail hunting takes place on private property.

There are hardly any public hunting lands in South Texas. Hunting on private properties is available only to those who own the land, are invited to hunt by the owner or manager, those who lease hunting rights from the owner, or those who hunt with outfitters and guides.

Finding a good place to hunt in the Brush Country is not an easy or inexpensive chore. Hunting leases are generally expensive, as are "package" or guided hunts. The cost of the latter start at about $2,500 and go up, depending upon the ranch and the amenities offered with the hunt. Even so, package hunts are becoming increasingly popular. They are also highly successful if you do your homework before selecting an outfitter. Remember, just because you book a hunt in Texas south of a line from Victoria northwest to San Antonio and west to Del Rio, does not ensure you the opportunity at a good buck. The quality of the hunt and the animals available vary greatly from ranch to ranch.

Guides hunt their clients in a variety of ways from hunting safari style (cruising ranch roads until an animal is spotted), to hunting from permanent blinds, to still-hunting and rattling. Should you decide to go on a guided hunt in Texas, as anywhere, pay attention to what your guide says and follow his suggestions on how to hunt a particular area. If you have enough faith in someone to pay him for the privilege of hunting on his land or with his hunting operation, have enough faith in your outfitter/guide to follow his suggestions or leads when it comes to hunting on his home turf.

The desert-like Brush Country of southern Texas and northern Mexico offers great opportunities for the serious whitetail hunter.

171

I have hunted deer in the Brush Country and similar habitat in a great variety of ways. As you may have guessed from statements in previous chapters, my favorite way to hunt whitetails in the Brush Country is a combination of still-hunting and rattling. I also enjoy hunting from highly mobile tripod stands. Tripods allow you to move into an area and set up to hunt for three or so days, then move to a new area, without greatly disturbing the local deer. Tripods take the place of climbable tree stands in brushy country, since there are few if any trees large enough to climb in the region.

Challenging Old Bucks

During my early years of hunting the Brush Country I often picked out one or two deer I wanted to hunt each year. These were generally bucks that were mature, or over-the-hill bucks that had big antlers and had survived several hunting seasons. I learned about them from other hunters or ranch personnel. The older mature deer can truly be a challenge to hunt and possibly take. I eventually took some of the old bucks, but certainly not all! However, in hunting them I learned much about hunting deer in South Texas' Brush Country and similar habitats throughout the whitetail's range.

Patterning deer, especially mature bucks, is not an easy chore. Nor is it often successful, unless you have large parcels of land to hunt and can hunt early in the season. Research conducted in the Brush Country of South Texas shows some bucks may have a home range as large as 10,000 acres. Some bucks have a spring and summer range, and then move to another area to spend the fall and early winter. Still others simply roam throughout a huge area. Other bucks may be in an area for a while, but then move to a new area. And, yes, some bucks have a small area in which they live. I am convinced those bucks that live within a small area are those that are never or rarely ever seen by hunters or anyone else. Some bucks are masters at evading hunters. Remember also, white-tailed bucks are quite simply individuals. They may follow certain trends, but do not make the mistake of thinking whitetails all behave in a similar manner. To do so will likely leave you wondering if there is anything besides young bucks wherever you hunt. This is true in the Brush Country or anywhere else whitetails roam.

One of the ranches I managed for a while in South Texas was home to several good bucks. The ranch was high-fenced and comprised nearly 15,000 acres–well over 20 square miles. It was rather long and relatively narrow, varying from a mile to three miles wide. For several years, each early fall we saw a buck in the southwest corner of the ranch, easily identified because of a large white spot on his shoulder. As soon as the rut approached he moved to the far northeast corner of the ranch, a little over 12 air miles away. When the rut was over he would start moving back to where he spent the spring and summer. We watched the buck make this seasonal shift for four years. I say "watched," but our observations were limited. Had it not been for an early and late helicopter game survey and a few hunter observations, we would never have known what the deer did. After four years the buck simply disappeared. I suspect he was killed by coyotes or a mountain lion that frequently drifted through the ranch.

Bucks, as I mentioned, are individuals. I have seen Brush Country bucks walk in a relatively straight line like they were on a mission. Where possible I have followed some of these bucks for quite a distance, sometimes as far as six to eight miles. In each instance when I spotted or followed such a buck they were already on their way. Where they had come from or how far they had already come, I do not know. When I left them, due to their crossing into property I did not have access to, they were still walking as if they were on a designated mission. How far they went, where, or for what purpose, I am unsure.

Lessons Of The Watertrap Buck

I have also seen bucks that primarily lived in a relatively small area most of their lives. Several years ago I managed a large ranch for whitetails and livestock. In the far southeast corner of the ranch was a "water trap," essentially a water windmill and water trough that were fenced so we could trap cattle when they came to drink. The water trap was about 400 acres in size.

The first time I saw this particular buck we were rounding up cattle. We jumped him from a thicket as we moved through it on horses. When we did, all thoughts of the cattle were forgotten. There was little doubt the buck with 12 long typical points and about a 24-inch spread would make the Boone and Crockett record book. Unfortunately, we saw him only briefly. That fall we started hunting the buck. He was not seen again until after the hunting season when we conducted our post-season game survey.

The following summer one of the ranch hands reported seeing the buck several times as the animal was developing his antlers. A few weeks before the opening of the hunting season I conducted a spotlight game survey in the small pasture to census the population there, but also to see if I could find the big buck. We spotted him near the windmill, again only briefly. That brief look at him, however, confirmed he was as big as the year before. When hunting season opened we started hunting the buck. He was not to be found.

About midway through the season we worked cattle in the trap, using a helicopter. We jumped the buck near the windmill. For the rest of the season the hunters on the property sat in the windmill, staying there from daylight to dark. The buck was never seen. Occasionally the ranch hands reported seeing him in the same area, after the season closed. I was convinced the buck was so intimately knowledgeable of his home area, he simply would be impossible to take by hunting.

We hunted that buck for four hunting seasons and hunted him hard. Yet during that time he was never seen by a hunter. When he was seen during the hunting season it was by ranch personnel and it was always in the same spot. Several of the hunters on the property tried

With a lack of large trees, highly mobile tripods are ideal for hunting brushy country habitats.

their best to pattern the buck. I am convinced the buck learned to pattern them better than they patterned him. I have seen this same thing happen again and again.

The old buck eventually died. We found his skull, one antler still attached, but the other recently shed. He had been a worthy opponent and I was saddened by his passing.

When hunting in the Brush Country it is not uncommon to see a deer one time and then never see him again. I realize the same takes place nearly anywhere whitetails are hunted. I am also convinced there are many bucks no one ever sees.

From personal observations of dealing with a lot of different mature bucks, it seems to me if a buck can survive to be four years old or older, his chances of surviving to a ripe old age are greatly increased. Therein lies one of the great joys of hunting in the Brush Country. On many ranches in South Texas only a relatively small percentage of the bucks available are taken each year by hunting. Many other bucks are given the opportunity to survive.

In previous chapters I have related how to hunt whitetails using rattling horns and how to hunt senderos, both typical hunting techniques used in brushy habitat. My co-author, Bill Bynum, has done similarly. I have often stated that "a white-tailed deer is a white-tailed deer, is a white-tailed deer, is a white-tailed deer...." While deer behave in somewhat of a similar manner no matter where they live, they are still individuals. It's been said before but it certainly bears repeating. The hunting techniques used in different habitats may need to be modified if you expect to be successful. The principles may be the same, but the applications may be a little different.

In some areas of the country deer drives are popular. But mention deer drives in the Brush Country and most of the local hunters will laugh in your face. However, that does not mean they will not work.

Weather in southern habitats is fickle. One day it may be cold, but the next day a hot spell might move right on in. Several years ago several friends and I hunted a ranch just above the Rio Grande in some of the best deer country in Texas. We scheduled our hunt according to when we hoped would be the ideal time to take advantage of the rut and, hopefully, some cool weather.

When the day of the hunt finally arrived, the cool weather we anticipated did not happen! Instead of normal daily temperatures in the 40s to 70s, it was in the high 90s. We hunted early in the morning by sitting in tripods overlooking feeding and watering areas. We rattled antlers, sat in windmills, sat in areas watching thick brush, and wide open areas. Regardless of what we did the results were always the same, no deer! We knew the property held some of the biggest bucks in the Brush Country, yet we simply could not find any of them–not even mature bucks with little antlers. Even the does quit moving as the temperature increased. Unfortunately, in recent years this type of weather seems to have become the norm, rather than the exception in southern Texas.

Driving South Texas Bucks

At wits' end, we organized a deer drive and began by pushing small thickets. After setting up standers, the pushers started moving through the thick thornbush. Making noise was not a problem. Not only were the pushers breaking branches, you could also keep up with them by the frequent cries of "Ouch!" as they walked into thorns. The results of the drives were interesting. We chased out a considerable number of javelinas, wild hogs, coyotes, and rabbits, but no deer. The pushers saw a few deer, but the ones they saw simply doubled back and disappeared in the thornbrush behind them.

After several unsuccessful drives while the temperatures were in the high 90s we all decided to go swimming rather than hunting, well, at least during the heat of the day. Two days later a cold front blew in and we were practically overrun with bucks. We saw bucks no matter how we hunted. That is deer hunting in the Brush Country!

Deer drives can occasionally work in the Brush Country. But the successful ones that I have been involved with were comprised of only two people, one pusher and one hunter. Back in the early 1980s I managed a large ranch just north of Laredo. The hunting rights on the property were leased by a friend who had hunted throughout the world, but had never taken a good whitetail. On the ranch lived a wide typical 11 point buck, wide as in having at least a 26-inch spread with long tines.

The buck lived on a low ridge that was bordered on either side by low-growing mesquite and prickly pear cactus. The top of the ridge was primarily comprised of blackbrush and spiny hackberry, both ideal deer browse and cover. A wet cold front had blown through the area, making it so wet we could not get to the part of the ranch we normally hunted. However, camp was within easy walking distance of where the wide buck lived. Thus I sent the hunter to the north end of the ridge, via the open country and told him where to set up and wait. A couple of hours later I started making my push. Starting at the south end of the ridge I slowly still-hunted my way back and forth across the low ridge. Several times I saw little bucks and does ahead of me. They moved to the edge of the thicket then quickly ducked back in, all the while moving toward the hunter. About half way to the end of the nearly mile long ridge, I spotted the wide 11 point just as I walked to the edge of the thick brush where it gave way to the low brush. For a moment I thought he would break and run across it. If he did, I was going to shoot. If he did not, I was going to try to continue pushing him toward the hunter.

The buck walked back into the taller brush. I continued to zig and zag across the ridge, which was about 100 yards wide. A little closer to the end of the ridge I again saw the buck, this time on the other side of the ridges. Apparently he was doing basically the same thing I was, zigging and zagging across the ridge and staying only about 50 to 100 yards ahead of me. I hoped he would continue doing the same. If he did, the hunter would have an excellent opportunity to take the wide buck.

As I started nearing the end of the ridge I slowed down. Five minutes later I heard a loud shot nearby. Hearing only one, I was sure my friend

Larry Weishuhn with his 26-inch wide basic eight point, taken at high noon in the Brush Country.

had taken the big buck. I took off at a run. After only about 100 yards I came upon the shooter. He was shaking his head and looked like he was about to cry. I listened as he told his tale of woe.

The wide buck had walked out within 25 steps of him. He looked briefly in my friend's direction and then started watching his back trail. The sight of the deer, especially with the buck looking away from him and making the animal's 26-inch wide rack look like 40 inches, was too much. My friend, who had coolly shot charging African lions and elephants, was completely unnerved at the sight of a "lowly" white-tailed buck. He missed!

I have had the same thing happen to me. Quite a few years ago I was hunting in the Brush Country, just as the bucks were really beginning to come to rattling horns. The weather was warm and foggy to the point where we could only see ahead about 20 yards. Shortly after starting a rattling sequence I spotted what almost looked like a ghost. A "form" started moving toward me. Intently I peered through the fog but could only make out that it was probably a deer. It took several minutes for the apparition to take the form of a white-tailed buck. Immediately my heart started beating at a rapid pace. The buck's neck was swollen but I could not really make out the size of his rack. I could tell he was definitely a mature buck, but I could not see his antlers clearly. I suspected he had to be big. After all, I was hunting on a ranch known for huge white-tails. Now seeing what might be a monster, to say the least, I was primed. The buck moved a little closer and disappeared behind a clump of prickly pear. I raised my rifle and got ready just in case it was the kind of buck I was looking for. Suddenly the buck's antlers appeared on the right side of the prickly pear clump. Hurriedly I counted five points on each side, plus his main beam. A typical twelve point, just like I have longed for since I could remember. I started shaking. My knees and lower lip started quivering. There was a metallic taste in my mouth, then it grew exceedingly dry. When the buck finally walked from behind the prickly pear and out of the fog, at 15 yards I shot, but only in the direction of the deer. I was so excited I totally blew the opportunity. I probably missed the buck by a good six to eight feet! Big bucks do strange things to people!

On other occasions I have been more "composed." However, I have to admit hunting in the Brush Country gets me excited, especially when there is an opportunity to hunt and take a monstrous buck.

Midday Socials

One of the best bucks I have ever taken, a 26-inch wide eight point that missed making the record book by only a narrow margin, was taken in the Brush Country. I had seen the deer in the previous year while hunting with John Wootters and a couple of other friends. But I had seen him only briefly after dark in the headlights as we were driving back to camp. The deer had also been seen and photographed by a helicopter pilot as he worked cattle on the ranch. Thus I knew of his existence. However, other than that one sighting, I did not know where to start hunting for the buck since the pilot would not divulge where he had seen the deer.

Larry Weishuhn with a wide nine point buck taken on the Perlitz Ranch in South Texas, while hunting with Bill Whitfield and the "Realtree Outdoors" video crew.

By the time I could finally find time to hunt the ranch, it was after the end of the peak of the rut. I drove to the ranch in the dark. Shortly after daylight I rattled up three young bucks first try and two more bucks about a quarter of a mile away on my second attempt. The rest of the morning was spent still-hunting along the edge of a ridge overlooking a brushy creek bottom. I had previously seen several good bucks in the area. However, it was not to be this morning.

Just before noon I drove back to camp to see if my companions, who were driving in from various other camps, had arrived. They had not and I decided to go hunt another area before checking back at camp later. I drove my Jeep Cherokee to an area where, in the past, we had always seen quite a few does—an area my friend Steve Warner describes as a "social area." I was not disappointed. As soon as I peered over the slight rise I spotted 12 does, feeding in a loose-knit group. Off to the right I spotted a buck. He had long tines and was fairly massive. He was certainly a good deer, that I could tell. I glanced at my watch. It was just before noon. The night before the moon had been full. Quite frankly I had expected to see deer during the middle of the day, based on past experiences.

I looked back at the buck just as he turned to walk away. The adrenaline rush I experienced at that sight was almost overwhelming! The long-tined buck looked as if he was 30 inches wide. Making a long story short, I shot the buck with my .309 JDJ Contender handgun. At the shot the buck went down so quickly I was afraid I had missed and he had disappeared. Hurriedly and excitedly I ran toward where he had stood. Then I saw his rack, poking out of the tall grass. For a while I just stood there, shaking. Several moments later I stood admiring a monstrous eight point buck.

I have long been a proponent of hunting during the middle of the day. As a biologist and as a hunter I have seen more big bucks during the middle of the day than at any other time. This is especially the case in hunting Brush Country whitetails. Recently, while hunting with Jim Raney of Brush Country Guide Service in Mexico, I noticed the same thing. What big bucks I saw during the trip were seen during the midmorning to midafternoon. Numerous times in years past as a biologist I checked on hunting camps. I drove in about the middle of the day because I knew the hunters would be in camp. While driving in, I would see many big bucks. Some would be feeding, others would be chasing does, still others were simply roaming.

In camp, quite often I listened to the laments of hunters about a lack of deer in the area. For the longest time I did not mention what I had seen on my way to their camp—I simply filed away the information.

Why big bucks, especially those in the Brush Country, move during the middle of the day is a mystery to me. There are those who contend middle-of-the-day movement is a normal thing deer do. Yet those same researchers state deer move only, or primarily right after daylight and right before dark. There are also those who say big bucks move during the middle of the day because they have learned to pattern hunters. Most of us hunt early and late; our movements are predictable. Breaking from this norm might just give the hunter that slight edge he keeps looking for. As for me, I will always hunt midday, but I will also hunt early and late. I have often said I hunt a lot, but I never get to hunt quite as much as I really want to. Hunting midday simply increases both the amount of time spent afield and our opportunities at taking a really good buck.

Given the choice of only being able to hunt whitetails in North America in one area, my choice would definitely be the Brush Country.

Chapter 15

Hunting The Farm Lands

Bill Bynum

The sun was slowly setting as I sat nestled in the thick honeysuckle. This natural blanket of foliage would guard me from the keen eyes of any deer. These were my youthful thoughts as I began scanning the large cornfield. Within minutes, I thought, the buck of my dreams would appear from the nearby cedar thicket, enter the field, and begin feeding on the corn. When the buck began his feeding, I would slowly aim my shotgun. The single-shot 12 gauge would send my slug straight and true. Yes sir, I knew I was about to become a full-fledged deer hunter.

That day ended like countless others over the past 30-something years. I slowly walked home in the dark wondering why the deer did not appear. It simply did not make any sense that the deer did not come to the cornfield to feed. These were my youthful thoughts at the time.

Times have changed since the days of my youth. Through the years I have discovered many interesting things about farmland deer hunting, and the habits of the white-tailed deer. I have also learned farmland hunting is more than taking ambush beside a cornfield. There are many elements pertaining to developing a farmland hunting strategy. One such element is, in most cases, farmlands provide the three essential requirements (food, water, and cover) deer need. This can be related to many farms having domestic livestock.

Farms that have no livestock will primarily produce some form of agricultural crop. These crops can also attract and contain deer within the farm's boundaries.

I have learned there are foods deer like, other than corn. I have also learned why deer sometimes prefer corn over some of those other foods. Having the privilege to grow up on a farm has helped me in learning about farmland deer. Though there may be some differences in comparing one farm to another, there are some common factors, as well. One such factor is that all farms have an owner!

You And The Landowner

Before any farm can be properly hunted, landowner permission *must* be acquired. This not only makes things right for all ethical hunters, but

Farmlands can be productive when hunted properly. Here hunters plan a farmland strategy.

Landowner permission is a must! Landowners can also be helpful in locating key hunting areas.

makes hunting more fun. Another valuable aspect of gaining landowner permission is the information that can be acquired from the landowner. Often hunters will discover the landowner to be more than cooperative in giving information that can save time in locating the primary areas, information that could lead the hunter to the biggest buck on the farm. This is the reason I try to stay in year-round contact with the landowner.

Farmers work hard and lending a helping hand with some of the chores never hurts. Being able to deplete some of the predators from the farm can also be a bonus. This not only aids the landowner, but can strengthen the deer herd.

Knowing The Farm

I cannot emphasize the importance of knowing the hunting habitat. To better understand the given habitat, extensive scouting must be performed. Much of this was discussed in Chapter 5.

Experience has taught me other factors are important to farmland hunting. One such factor is the seasonal cycle of most farms.

In most of the southern states, farmlands are constantly changing. This is due to the rotation of agricultural crops. Other food sources (mast) found upon farmlands are also changing quickly during the hunting periods. Knowing where to find both soft and hard mast foods are important.

Many times hunters discover some form of mast is the key to success-ful hunting. Wise hunters take note: Some mast crops are limited in quan-tity. This means these limited sources will be consumed quickly by the deer. This can be true of some of the soft mast crops found in the south-ern United States.

Soft Mast Success

A few years ago I was nestled high in a large cedar tree waiting for a deer to come by. It was the middle of archery season (October) and the weather was mild. I had been forced to abandon my previous hunting site, a soybean field. The change in location was due to the soybeans drying, and therefore, not seeing any deer. This day would mark three consecutive days of hunting a clover field. The clover field revealed numerous deer tracks around the wooded edges. Sadly, I had not seen any of the tracks' creators. I was now wondering if all the deer had aban-doned the farm.

My thoughts were soon answered when a small buck suddenly appeared across the field. Though the deer was safe, I still got a little excited just seeing one. With this surge I quickly retrieved my binocular and began spying on the buck.

Minutes passed as I watched the animal feed in one particular loca-tion. During this time I wondered why the clover was better there than near my stand. This became apparent as the deer suddenly stood upright on its back legs. From this position I could see the deer extend its neck before returning to all four legs. This occurred several times before I realized the critter was picking persimmons from the lower tree limbs.

Later, after the deer left, I went to examine the persimmon tree. What I discovered was shocking! The ground beneath the tree was a solid mass of tracks. Actually, the ground was torn up from the deer that had been there.

Examination of the area showed me the closest tree stand position was out of range for my bow; therefore, I elected to do the next best thing—find another persimmon tree. This was easily accomplished by reviewing my scouting records and map of the farm since I had marked numerous persimmon trees on the map. The tree I located was on the edge of an abandoned field.

Less than 20 yards from the persimmon tree was a nice-sized oak tree. It would serve as my stand location as the oak leaves would conceal my human outline.

Soon my portable tree stand was in position and it was time to prepare the persimmon tree. Preparation of the persimmon tree was quickly accomplished by vigorously shaking the tree. The shaking placed a gen-erous portion of the fruit on the ground. Next I took a handful of persim-mons and smashed them into the bark of the tree. This allowed a strong scent of the fruit to flow around the area. With some luck, I would lure a nice buck to the persimmon tree the next morning.

Dawn of the next morning found me nestled in my portable tree stand. The heavy frost made the air feel more refreshing than normal. It was also the heavy frost that silhouetted the deer feeding at the base of the persimmon tree.

Long moments elapsed as I watched the deer browse around the tree. Daylight was rapidly approaching and I knew I could make positive identification soon.

Within minutes the small rack of the buck was identified and my pulse rate returned to normal. For nearly 15 minutes, I watched the little buck feed on the persimmons. The buck was nothing more than a four pointer. I wanted something better and elected to enjoy the show.

Perhaps another quarter hour passed before the little buck suddenly came to attention. Like a statue the deer stood staring into the hardwoods. This action alerted me to the presence of another buck coming to the persimmon tree.

The sight of the six point buck was simply breathtaking. The animal was beautiful with the new sunlight reflecting off its slick body. The buck's rack was not the most impressive I had ever seen, but it was a rack. This was not a factor as I was hunting for meat and not antlers.

Minutes passed by as I waited for the buck to begin feeding on the persimmons. Ever so slowly did the deer begin to feed as the lesser buck moved away. I felt some sympathy for the smaller buck as it retreated to the woods. Now it was my time to become the dominant figure of the area.

With the buck now presenting a broadside shot for me, I began raising my bow. Slowly I began drawing the bowstring as all my concentration focused upon the deer's shoulder. This act of instinctive shooting was completed as my anchor point was felt. Again my actions were automatic as I released the arrow from the bow.

The bright colors of the arrow's fletch quickly disappeared on the buck's shoulder. It was at this moment I heard the sound of the broadhead connecting as the deer reacted. With the loud smacking sound of the arrow connecting, the deer suddenly dropped to the ground. The buck's response was only momentary as it quickly leaped and bounded for the woods.

The animal's reaction sent a surge of excitement through me. I knew my shot had been good and I was happy. Then, taking a deep breath, I heard a crashing sound from the woods. I knew the hunt was successful only upon locating the deer.

In minutes I retrieved my arrow only inches from where the buck had stood. With complete penetration it was easy to follow the animal's trail. In less than 15 minutes I was admiring my trophy, a trophy I might not have taken if not for knowing the animal's habitat.

Hunters will also discover other soft mast foods can be potential hot spots. Some of the soft mast crops I refer to are flowering dogwood trees, crabapples, American elders, and wild grapes. As stated, there are numerous soft mast crops found in the southern states. Locating all the preferred foods and scouting will lead the hunter to success.

Bill Bynum displays his buck. Though not a large rack, the buck presented an exciting hunt.

The Ever Changing Habitat

Changes in farm management can and will affect the animal's habits; therefore, it is important for hunters to know how these changes influence deer. It is this knowledge that will help the hunter to form a hunting strategy. Knowing where to find the preferred food sources during a given time period is one of the key factors. Hunters must remember food is vital to the deer and to successful hunting.

Deer, unlike some humans I know, eat wisely! Over 500 different types of foods deer will eat can be found in the southern United States. Some of these foods are the primary agricultural crops of North America. With this information, much of what we are about to read can be applied anywhere. But some factors should be considered before trying to locate everything a deer can eat.

One factor is that deer are usually selective in their feeding. Like most humans, deer have preferences in what they eat. Unlike humans who usually base preference upon taste, deer are not as finicky. Deer mainly base their preference on their body's needs and will often select foods based on the protein or carbohydrate content.

The amount of the food's content can and will vary with the time of year. This is why it is important to know when certain foods are at their nutritional peaks. These peak periods will vary according to the geographic location. Naturally, the growing seasons of the various food sources differ from state to state. Hunters knowing which foods are at their peaks may discover hunting hot spots.

In most states hunters using archery equipment will be the first afield. Experienced bow hunters know most hunting strategies will focus on the deer's feeding habits. Many times deer will concentrate on one food source more than another.

Archery seasons usually begin in the latter days of summer when most plant life is still green. During this time period, deer are feeding heavily on foods high in protein. Protein is needed for growth and muscle development. This feeding phase will not stop until the early days of winter. Until the deer's body needs change, the animal will continue to eat the foods he needs. One of the greatest food sources found for producing protein is the soybean. The soybean is one of the most common of southern agricultural crops.

Deer love to feed on the green leaves of the soybean plant. Feeding will begin in the plant's early stage and continue until the plant has dried. Bow hunters will discover that anywhere soybeans are located, deer will be nearby. This is the reason I place a lot of emphasis on using this food source during the early days of archery season. In fact, I rely heavily on soybean areas for much of my early season hunting. Many of the tactics I use were discussed in Chapter 13.

Now let's review some other important farmland foods.

Whole Kernel Whitetails

Corn is one of the South's top agricultural cash crops. Corn can be found almost anywhere there is farmland. I feel there would be little

Among preferred foods the soybean is one of the deer's favorite.

debate that corn is one of the whitetail's favorite foods. From the time the plant sprouts from the ground, deer will eat it. Deer will nip off the tip of the stalk as quickly as it begins to grow. They will eat the milky kernels as they develop until they have dried hard.

Corn is a food source that is high in carbohydrates. This is important for hunters to know as carbohydrates help produce body heat. This can be an important factor in developing a hunting strategy for farmlands.

Due to the seasonal time period, corn will have little effect on a hunting strategy until it has dried. This is because farmers harvest the corn from the field once it dries. With this information, hunters should realize it will be the corn left in the field after harvesting that will attract the animals; therefore, it will be the fields containing the highest amount of unharvested corn that will be best for hunting. This is especially true if substantial cover is nearby.

Cornfields bordering areas of adequate cover can become potential hot spots. These hot spots will occur during certain weather conditions, such as sudden temperature changes. An abrupt decline in temperatures

The cornfield in the background produced this buck for Bill Bynum's young son.

can be shocking to the deer's body. Hunters realizing this can take advantage of the change in temperatures. Here's why:

When temperatures suddenly drop, deer need to generate body heat quickly. As stated, corn is high in carbohydrates. With this information we should see why cornfields become potential hot spots. From past experience, I have found deer to begin feeding heavily on corn 24 hours before the temperature starts to decline.

Wise hunters will always monitor the weather and be prepared for these weather conditions. It is also a wise move to spend every minute possible in the stand during changing conditions. Some of the best bucks I have taken were during the midday hours during a weather change. Experienced hunters know the key to harvesting trophy bucks is to be where they are. A dedicated hunter will remain in the stand all day if necessary.

Of all the types of deer hunting terrain there are, farmland hunting is possibly the best. This is especially true for harvesting record book class deer. These deer are usually labeled as the "True Trophies." Though I do not completely agree with what is a true trophy, I do agree farmlands are the best for hunting such animals.

Farmlands have the potential for creating what is needed for growing big bucks. This is especially true if all the needed essentials are present. The essentials I refer to are abundant food sources, good genetics, and age. Without these three important factors, record book bucks cannot be produced.

Today many southern hunters lease or rent farmland for hunting. This practice helps the hunter as well as the farmer. The hunter receives land to hunt on, while the farmer receives the much-needed cash.

Many hunters lease farmland with high hopes of harvesting a record book buck. Each year a small percentage of hunters do fulfill this dream. Unfortunately, many do not because the animal simply doesn't exist on the farm.

This is why it is important for hunters to investigate farmland before leasing it. When investigating farmland, I get all the facts pertaining to the land for the previous five years, as I believe a buck must reach the age of three years before maturing.

Prospective leasers should also know the type of foods that have been available for at least five years prior to leasing. This will give some indication of minerals that have been provided for antler development of the residing animals. Knowing the history of the animals that have been harvested annually is also important, especially the number of bucks and their ages. If numerous young bucks have been taken annually, the odds are low for record book bucks. This information can also provide knowledge to the genetics of deer in the area.

Without a good genetic pool within the area, the chances are reduced for monster bucks. This is becoming a problem for many areas in the southern states. As I am not a biologist, I cannot make this recommendation on a scientific basis, but as a hunter, I feel the possibility of overharvesting is a different problem!

It takes a combination of factors to produce nice bucks such as this one.

Another factor that can affect a given area are poachers. These scumbags rob everyone involved in ethical deer hunting. This problem can be corrected when all concerned parties get involved.

Without farmland hunting, a vast majority of deer hunting would be lost. This is the reason sound hunter/landowner relationships are important to the future of deer hunting.

Chapter 16

Rainy Day Bucks

Larry L. Weishuhn

I was drenched. I was so wet my boots "squished and squashed" with each and every step. My glasses were spotted with raindrops and I could hardly see through them. The wet and cold were starting to get to me and I was starting to shiver. But I was happy! Hunting season had finally arrived and I was going to make the most of the few days I had to hunt before going back to school. The rain had been falling steadily–well, actually, it was more of a downpour. I had tried to get out of it by standing under trees with low-hanging leafy branches. That worked for a little while, but then I started getting wet. The only rain gear I had to my name was bright yellow and I was not about to wear anything such as that into the deer woods. Someone might see me and laugh. Even worse, I would be seen shining like a beacon in the night to deer that might wander by.

Just as I shifted my weight from one foot to the other, I caught movement in the huckleberries to my left. It was a deer. All thoughts of wet and cold were quickly forgotten. Moments later the young buck walked into an open area. I raised my old Model 340 Savage bolt action chambered for the .30-30 Winchester, wiped the accumulated raindrops from the old scope, and shot the young buck squarely through the shoulder at a distance of less than 40 yards. As soon as he went down I started whooping and hollering. To say I was elated would have been the understatement of the year. At the moment I did not even notice the downpour!

That rainy day happened many years ago when I was growing up and hunting only a few hundred yards behind our house in rural Texas in the Zimmerscheidt Community. Back then, if I hunted in the rain I simply got wet. During those early days the only rain gear I had was a yellow slicker that was normally tied behind my saddle. I preferred that it stay there when I hunted. Both rain gear and I have come a long way since back then.

Movement at the edge of the rain-blocked opening interrupted my thoughts and brought me back to the present. From where I sat in my tripod overlooking a prickly pear flat surrounded by mesquites, I watched a young buck materialize out of the watery distance. He walked to one of the mesquites and started his scraping routine. Earlier I had noticed

Rain affects deer differently in different regions and habitats.

there were numerous scrapes in the immediate area. The rain continued to fall, making me appreciate the 10x rain gear I wore all the more.

Proper Clothing Makes Hunting In Rain Easier

The advent of new high-tech materials such as Gore-Tex and many others allows modern rain gear to keep out rain, while allowing perspiration to escape. Such a combination makes hunting in the rain almost comfortable. Because of the variable fall weather we experience in the South, I keep rain gear in my day pack, just in case a downpour should occur while I am in the field. Rain no longer affects me, other than my being unable to see through rain-specked lenses. How it affects deer is something else.

I have learned rain has varied effects on deer movement in the South. In some areas when it rains, deer simply seem to disappear completely. In other areas rainfall seems to increase deer activity.

Deer that lived in the area where I grew up, in the wooded gravel hills on the edge of the Gulf Coast Prairie, seemed to be affected very little by rainfall. They seemed to be no more or less active than they were during other types of weather. But that is not the case everywhere.

Alabama Deer And Rain

I have often hunted in Alabama, a state I love to visit. But, it seems my hunting trips only take place when it rains there. On my first trip to that

Georgia resident, Bob Thompson, quietly and slowly hunts along the edge of an oak bottom.

state, I hunted with J. Wayne Fears. Wayne is one of the most respected biologists and writers in the country, certainly one for whom I have the utmost respect. During that initial trip to his home state we hunted some of the best lodges in Alabama, but I never saw a buck and only a few does. Throughout the trip it rained, every single day. During that same trip several rivers flooded. I would have thought the rising water would have driven deer out of the bottoms. I was wrong! Wayne had warned me that if it rained my chances of taking a deer would be greatly diminished. He told horror stories of having a lodge full of hunters when it rained back when he ran Westervelt Lodge and later several of his own Back Country Lodges. When the rain started, deer movement totally ceased in the areas they hunted. The day before such rain or the day after there were plenty of deer to be seen. But the days it rained it seemed the deer crawled into holes and covered themselves up with whatever local vegetation or soil was available.

He and I hunted those same areas when we hunted together that first trip. Where a few days previously other hunters had been seeing 10 to 20 deer a day, we saw no deer at all! I could hardly believe it.

Deer in that area of Alabama obviously crawl into a thicket and stay there when it rains. They do not venture forth until it stops. On that particular trip the only deer seen were those spotted when it finally stopped raining one afternoon for about an hour. During that same trip Eddie Salter, of wild turkey calling fame, joined us for a couple of days. Eddie, too, struck out, in spite of trying every imaginable trick he could to find deer, including doing some deer mini-drives. The only thing we got for our efforts was wet. Also, Eddie's pickup got mired in mud so badly that we needed a log sledder to get him back on solid ground.

In other areas of the Old South rainfall seems to have little effect on deer movement. Hunting in southern Georgia I have seen a great number of deer while it was misting rain, or, for that matter, pouring down. They began feeding when the rain started and continued doing so throughout the rainy afternoon. One of my Georgia bucks was taken while it was raining, which it had been doing since the previous day.

Well before daylight I crawled into my tree stand. Quickly I set up an umbrella over my stand, crawled under it, and waited for enough light to see. The morning came gray, dingy, and dank, complete with occasional mist interrupted by hard rain showers. I vividly remembered my rainy day experiences in Alabama and wondered if I were going to be in for the same. Nonetheless this time I was comfortable and dry, with the exception of my glasses. Those I occasionally wiped clean so I could see.

The first deer I saw were a doe and her fawn. They fed on some white oak acorns until they had their fill, then laid down less than 20 yards from my stand. Ten minutes after those first deer laid down I spotted three more does and two fawns. They, too, fed on acorns. A short time later three more does appeared. I had deer all around me. Thankfully I was sitting quietly about 20 feet above them. I hoped the height advantage would keep them from scenting me. I watched the various deer, doing my best to grow a set of antlers on every one of them. Just then I heard a deer grunting. I turned in the direction of the sound and spotted a young buck heading my way–well, actually, in the direction of the biggest bunch of does. He came toward them in typical rutting buck behavior, his head low to the ground as if trailing. The first doe he came to looked at him, giving him that hard stare indicating she was not the least bit interested in his advances. The buck got the message and headed toward another. This doe also simply paid him no mind, totally ignoring his advances. Immediately he switched to yet another doe. This one turned tail and started to run, but stopped long enough to urinate before leaving. The buck stopped, smelled the urine, and immediately picked up her trail. The two disappeared into the maze of briars, brambles, and regrowth three-year-old pine adjoining the stand of oaks where I was hunting.

A few minutes passed. Then to my right about 75 yards away I saw a doe running in my direction. Right behind her came the buck. By then it was pouring down rain. The buck was not really all that big, but he fit my Georgia requirements. I try my best these days to only take mature deer. I strongly believed him to be at least four years old, even though his rack was not all that big. When the buck stopped in the road leading to my stand, I shot him. Thankfully he dropped in his tracks.

Hunting in pouring rain has its drawbacks. If you are not properly dressed or prepared, you will be wet as well as cold and miserable. But even worse is trying to track a wounded deer in the rain. Should you not immediately kill the deer in the pouring rain, there is always the possibility of losing him because the rain may wash away the blood trail. I once lost a good Brush Country whitetail, a basic massive 10 point with four kickers, in a blowing rainstorm. By the time I found him late that afternoon he had been nearly completely eaten by coyotes. All that remained were the major part of his skeletal system and his skull and rack. For this reason several southern camps with which I am associated do not allow bow hunting when it is raining hard. This is an ethical decision every bow hunter and gun hunter as well, must make.

Rain: How Much And How Long?

Throughout most of the South, it is not a question of whether or not it's going to rain during the hunting season, it is a question of how long and how much. Throughout the fall, weather and rain seem to simply go hand-in-hand. While I do not particularly like hunting in mist and rain, often I do not have any choice. My hunts are set up well in advance, sometimes over a year before. I cannot change my mind about hunting somewhere simply because of a little rain, or, for that matter, a lot of rain. The same is true for nearly any other weather condition. Regardless of what is thrown at me: rain, drought, wind, snow, extreme cold, or extreme heat, I am going to give it my best shot, even if it takes adjusting my hunting techniques considerably.

In other areas of the South, especially the southwest, rain seems to turn on deer. They move more than normal when it rains. Several years ago an old Mexican vaquero pulled me aside during a hunt south of the Rio Grande. He knew I was a wildlife biologist and loved hunting big

In Mexico a brush-wise vaquero told Larry Weishuhn big bucks like to walk in wet sand. He was right.

white-tailed bucks. "Señor Colorado (red in Spanish, and so named because of my red hair and beard), de muy grandes, day likes to walk in wet sand. It makes their feet feel *muy bueno!*" His prediction proved right. During our hunt everyone in camp ended up shooting a good buck in the rain. Most assuredly the local big bucks did enjoy walking in wet sand. Frankly, I have seen deer in other areas seem to enjoy walking in wet sand. I have talked to several hunters throughout the South who tell me that they have found places where there were exposed areas of sand that were covered with deer tracks. Some of the trails in these sandy areas led in circles so it's likely the deer truly did enjoy walking in wet sand. Why this occurs? Quen Sabe! I do not know. I only know that it happens.

One fall J. Wayne and Sherry Fears and I were invited to hunt the huge San Pedro Ranch near Carrizo Springs in southern Texas. The day we arrived it started misting rain. It continued raining for the next five days. During that time we all had many opportunities at big bucks. Wayne ended up taking the largest, a massive 10 point. He shot the buck with a Thompson/Center Contender with a custom barrel for the .338 JDJ. My buck and Sherry's buck were taken as they visited scrapes between rain showers. During the week of mist and rain we saw a tremendous amount of scraping activity. Each time the rains quit, the bucks freshened their scrapes. If this is a normal activity or one that was simply conducted by the local bucks under the rainy circumstances, I cannot say for certain. I only know that it happened. I have seen the same thing occur several times in other areas of the southwest.

Big Bucks Like Wet Sand

While on a hunt to Mexico, the one where I was told that big bucks like to walk in wet sand, the local vaquero showed me several large scrapes. Some were nearly a foot deep and had obviously been used for several years. He, too, mentioned that the local bucks tended to freshen their scrapes after each rain, during the rut.

One of the scrapes he showed me had a footprint in it that was huge. According to the vaquero the buck had a huge body, but only a relatively small 10 point rack. He suggested the buck would be a good one to take. He would make many delicious Christmas tamales, a tradition in that part of Mexico. According to the vaquero, it had been a long time since he and his family had been able to get any deer meat, not since the last hunting season. At that point I had been hunting another buck for several days and was ready to switch. Besides I had to get back to the states in a couple of days to spend Christmas at home. If I intended to take a Mexican deer I would have to do so fairly quickly.

The following morning I walked to a tripod I had set up during the night. The tripod overlooked a series of scrapes, the scrapes being used by the big-footed buck. The rain continued to fall, although now finally somewhat intermittently. Throughout the morning I saw three young bucks and two does. Rather than go in for lunch I ate a soggy sandwich, washed down with lukewarm coffee. Right after lunch I saw movement

Mike McMurray (in hat), Sherry Fears, Larry Weishuhn, and J. Wayne Fears show the results of several days of hunting in the rain in South Texas.

coming through the misty wall of rain. I could not see antlers at first, but I could see the deer was huge in body when he walked along the edge of a barbed wire fence. At about 150 yards he stopped and shook. In doing so I noticed he had fairly massive antlers, but with relatively short tines. I strongly suspected this was the deer my vaquero friend had been talking about. Hurriedly I replaced my binocular with my borrowed 7X61 rifle, cranked the variable scope as high as it would go, and tried to pick a spot through the mesquite and thorn bushes to send a bullet. Moments later I squeezed the trigger. The solid "whump" drifted back through the falling rain. Hit squarely through the shoulders, the buck dropped immediately. It took mere seconds for me to cover the nearly 125 yards to reach his side. The buck was huge by Mexican standards, huge of body that is–and of foot! His rack had 11 total points on main beams that spread to about 16 inches wide. His tines had broken tips, and his brows were broken off near their bases. There was no doubt the buck was old. His facial features showed age, as did his Roman nose. Later I checked his lower jaw and estimated him to be eight plus years old. When the vaquero rode up to help me pack my deer back to camp, he let out a whoop when he saw which deer it was. I swear I saw him drooling occasionally between verses of some song I did not fully understand, but knew it had something to do with Christmas and tamales. Back at camp the buck, weighed on cotton scales, showed a field dressed weight of 198 pounds.

Many hunters in southern Texas head back to camp when it rains. Unfortunately they do not realize the worth of hunting in such adverse conditions. But if you are serious about hunting do not overlook hunting when it rains, regardless of where you hunt and especially in South Texas.

Rattling In The Rain

A few seasons ago Steve Warner, a biologist friend who designed Bush-lan Camo, decided to stay in his tripod during a windy, hard raining day during the middle of December. The ranch he hunted was a good one, only a couple of miles north of the Rio Grande. It held a considerable number of mature bucks. His morning hunt had gone slow. He had seen only four does and a couple of yearling bucks. At one point he nearly decided to crawl down and start walking the long road back to camp. He had initially instructed us not to come pick him up until dark.

As much out of frustration as anything, about midday he started rattling horns, even though it was raining and the wind was blowing close to 20 miles per hour. Much to his surprise a buck responded almost before he pulled the rattling horns apart during his first sequence. Just as quickly a second buck appeared, this one bigger than the first. Throughout the rest of the afternoon he continued rattling horns in the driving wind and rain. Throughout the afternoon bucks continued to respond. After a while he lost count of the total number of bucks that responded. But according to Steve over 20 mature bucks responded, including one buck that was near record book quality and

A soggy Larry Weishuhn shows the results of hunting in the rain, when other hunters were back in camp where it was warm and dry.

had a long extra antler growing between his two normal antlers. Unfortunately that buck did not stay long or show much more than his rack and head before disappearing into the brush. A neighbor had told us of the buck. He had seen him in early November, but then the buck had disappeared.

Would I have considered rattling horns as Steve did, in the pouring rain and wind? Perhaps. I have occasionally rattled up bucks in the rain. Not often, but it does happen. I do, however, like to still-hunt and rattle when the ground and the vegetation around me are wet. The moisture allows me to move quietly. One fall while hunting down South it started raining the day Ron Porter, my retired New Mexico game warden friend, and I began our annual whitetail hunt. Just before first light, gray though it was, I set Ron near a remote food plot. I headed to a thick patch of brush where I had previously seen an interesting buck. When it finally got light enough to see, I started rattling horns. Twenty minutes later I stood up and started to move to a new area. In doing so I spotted the buck I had seen a few days before. He was walking toward me, probably being slow to respond to my horn rattling. Hurriedly I ducked behind a shrub and raised my Thompson/Center Contender chambered for the .30-30 Winchester. When the buck stopped at 25 yards to look for the source of the fight, I squeezed the trigger. The buck took two steps. He stopped momentarily and then crumpled to the ground. By the time I finished the field-dressing chores I was soaked.

Rainy day bucks are not always easy. And hunting in the rain is not always successful. As mentioned earlier, deer in various types of climate and habitats are affected differently by precipitation. But the same is true for any other kind of adverse weather condition. Cold weather does not always make deer move in the South. If it gets too cold, they simply "hole up" and wait for it to get warmer. When it gets extremely hot, as it can do when hunting down South, deer may find a cool, shady spot and stay there until it cools down. As hunters we have to learn to make the best of adverse conditions. Sometimes that means simply getting out and hunting regardless of whatever the weather brings us. Of all the variables we are faced with as hunters, weather is the one factor over which we have no control. That does not mean we cannot try to learn ways to take a negative situation and turn it around to our advantage. If all our efforts fail because of adverse weather conditions, then so be it. Maybe next time we will appreciate good hunting weather conditions all the more!

Chapter 17

Hunting Southern Swamp Bucks: Gray Ghosts Of The Cyprus

Bill Bynum

The swamplands of the southern United States have mystified people for centuries. Swamps represent areas filled with danger and uncertainty lurking everywhere. I think much of this perception has been the result

The swamplands of the South can produce some exciting moments for the serious deer hunter.

of some Hollywood productions: Swamp monsters emerging from the blackish waters, giant reptiles hidden beneath the seas of beautiful lily pads. Just the way some movie dudes reflect upon Spanish moss hanging from cyprus trees is ghastly.

Swamps: Excuses Or Opportunities

Swamps, in my opinion, reflect a totally different perspective. When I look upon a swamp I see an area filled with wildlife and begging for exploration. I also see an area that can produce some of the finest white-tailed deer hunting south of the Mason-Dixon line.

Spending most of my life in northwestern Tennessee has been rewarding for me. Within this region I have access to almost any type of hunting terrain one could want. From rolling hills and farmlands to dense pine forests and river bottom swamps, my native land has it all within minutes of my home.

I began hunting swamplands at an early age for waterfowl and small game animals. The white-tailed deer population was low during this time period so other critters were on my agenda. I learned many lessons while hunting these animals, lessons that would help me in the future.

My first encounter with a swampland deer came early one cold December morning. I was trying desperately to avoid getting a wet hip boot while wading to my duck blind. The task of staying dry quickly became a lost cause due to a beaver trail. The sudden shock of the cold water filling my boot made me freeze in my tracks momentarily. This reaction did not last long as I scurried for shallow water.

Within minutes I located a muskrat house and was emptying my boot of its cold contents. In the east the sky was showing signs of a new day and I knew I had to be on my way. It was at that moment when I stepped down from the rat's house that my life changed.

No sooner did I slide into the water when I heard a startling sound. For a brief moment I thought a herd of cattle was charging me through the water. Then I saw the culprits in the dim light of dawn as they came closer.

The first positive identification was the enormous rack of the leader. In seconds the massive rack of the buck was less than 10 feet from me as it splashed through the water. Behind the buck were another smaller buck and four does. The deer were quickly engulfed in the nearby cane thicket. Long moments passed while I stood in disbelief and listened to the deer fade away. The remainder of that morning was spent trying to duck hunt with deer on my mind. The sight of the big buck had me ready to trade the shotgun for my deer rifle. I was ready to begin hunting swampland deer.

The remainder of that deer season was spent with me wading around the swamp looking for ol' big boy. I never got to see that buck or any other deer that season. I did, however, learn a few things that I recorded for future reference–things that I thought would guide me to taking a swamp buck.

The sight of the big buck haunted my thoughts throughout the following year. I could hardly wait for summer to end and deer season to begin. A tingle of excitement ran through me when I thought of stalking the swamp with my bow and arrow. I was determined to harvest a deer from the swamp, and this determination led me to discover many valuable lessons relative to swamp hunting.

One of the greatest lessons I received was that the swamp had its own ways. Unlike the woodlands I was used to hunting, the swamp proved to be much different.

The weeks prior to hunting season found me spending all my spare time scouting. I scouted for all the obvious signs of the white-tailed deer, signs such as trails, rubs, etc. Hours were spent walking the outer parameters of the swamp searching for signs. Most of my scouting proved to be only good exercise while sloshing through the mud and water. In short, I had found only a few sets of deer tracks for my labors. I was now feeling the deer I had seen were somewhat of a fluke and I was wasting my time. And then it happened!

Only a couple of days before the opening day of archery season I returned to the swamp. I had come to the swamp not to look for deer, but hopefully to collect some squirrel meat. I had managed to take four fox squirrels from a large hickory tree. Like most hardwoods the tree was located only a few yards from the edge of the water. While I silently sat beneath the tree, I detected a familiar sound–the sound of rapidly splashing water, which was uncommon in the swamp.

I listened to the sound while my eyes scanned the innermost portion of the swamp. Its source was hidden in the mass of cane and small trees. The sound grew louder as I now stood in anticipation. In moments I knew the creators of the noise would be upon me. My thoughts proved to be correct as the first of six deer emerged from the cane grove. With the parting of the cane a splendid eight point buck appeared. Next was another eight pointer with a slightly smaller rack. This deer was quickly followed my a handsome seven point buck. The seven pointer carried extremely long tines upon his dark colored rack. The other three deer were also bucks. A small-racked six pointer and two fork horns soon followed from within the cane. Before me stood the first bachelor group of swamp deer I had ever seen. In the fading afternoon sunlight I watched them walk single file into the hardwoods and disappear.

Needless to say, this scenario worked on my youthful mind as I returned home. I could not understand why the deer had emerged from the swamp the way they had. I could understand why the animals would come to hardwoods for food. This was the time of day many deer embark on their nighttime feeding sprees. But if this was true, it meant the deer had bedded in the swamp. This led to another question. How could a deer bed down in the waters of a swamp without drowning?

Classroom To Swamp, Or Vice Versa

The following afternoon found me scurrying from the classroom to the swamp. No time was lost getting to where I had seen the deer the after-

Hunting swamps requires vigilant scouting from the hunter. Nothing should remain unexplored.

noon before. With the exception of crossing the path of a large and quickly deceased water moccasin snake, everything was like the evening before. Minutes ticked by as the sounds of buzzing insects and wood duck calls filled my ears. I watched the swamp transform from daylight to darkness as the sun slowly faded. In the dim light, I watched a raccoon rob a crawfish from the shore of the swamp. Life was changing in this vast and eerie land when I detected the sound I had been waiting for.

The erratic sound of disturbed water grew louder and louder behind the wall of cane. I knew within seconds the deer would emerge before my eyes. I remember wondering which one of the bucks would be leading the way. I also remember how I was planning the upcoming hunt–how I would be waiting in only two days to collect my first swamp buck as it stepped from the cane.

The memories of that afternoon still linger in my mind. I still recall how my heart stopped when the first deer stepped from the cane. The sight of that massive 12 pointer simply took away my breath. Never before had I seen a deer in the wild as beautiful as that one. The antlers of the buck were massive to my young eyes, with long tines as I had never seen before. As with the buck of my first encounter, this buck's antlers spread beyond the width of his ears. It was the buck that would make me the envy of all my friends.

Time felt at a standstill as I watched the buck and three does disappear into the hardwoods. I was full of excitement as I cautiously exited

Hunters must be alert for the cotton-mouth snake when hunting swampland. (Photo credit: Scott Shupe.)

Bow hunting the swamplands will test a hunter's skills.

the swamp. I would not return to my secret place until it was time to hunt.

I began the first day of archery season that year walking through a thick fog. The fog engulfing me was mixed with the final hour of darkness. The existing conditions had me somewhat disoriented as I slowly emerged on the edge of the swamp. With only the sound of croaking bullfrogs to guide me, I was becoming worried. I was worried that I would be unable to locate the position from where I had planned to hunt, and that the deer would escape in the swamp without me ever seeing them.

My fears increased quickly as I realized I was lost in the fog. As I traveled, the darkness of night was now yielding to the gray of dawn. Panic was spreading within me until I noticed a track in the mud. With the aid of my flashlight I inspected it closely. There was no question it was the track I had left on my last visit. I knew it would be these tracks that would lead me to my hunting site. In minutes I had traveled through the fog and was leaning against the hickory tree. Above, the sound of rustling leaves indicated the presence of a squirrel. Soon these sounds increased as more squirrels began their daily feeding. Little did I know these sounds would teach me a valuable lesson. Minutes had turned into an hour since I had taken my position. Boredom was setting in as I stared through the fog in vain. With the increasing light, visibility was enhanced, but sadly, it presented nothing new to my eager eyes.

Squirrel Watching

To this day I do not know what made me start watching the squirrels above me, but for as long as I hunt I will never forget the price I paid for being distracted; that price being the wide rack of my trophy buck disappearing into the cane. In the time it took for a squirrel to gather a nut and begin to feed on it, my buck was gone! Where the buck came from I have no idea. I remember standing in amazement watching two does follow the monarch.

My education in swamp hunting was quickly progressing. My overall education in deer hunting was also paying off. I knew the changing wind direction would not allow me to return to my usual hunting position.

The next few days found me scouting other areas of the swamp. I knew there had to be more deer there. I also knew there were some key factors to hunting these deer–factors that I would have to learn if I was to become successful.

From the extensive scouting, I located other areas where deer had traveled in and out of the swamp. These areas were recorded on a crude map I had drawn of the swamp. On the map I listed the locations and area landmarks. The landmarks consisted of large cypress trees, small patches of water oaks, beaver houses, etc. In observing the landmarks, I realized all the travelways had something in common. That common denominator was water depth.

Having duck hunted and fished in the swamp for years, I knew the areas containing the water oaks were shallower than the surrounding waters. In many cases these areas consisted of the higher grounds before the swamp was created by the backwaters of the river. With this theory, I obtained some topographical maps of the swamp and began searching. In days I had located numerous areas where the deer were traveling. I also located the areas where I felt the deer were traveling to inside the swamp; areas of the highest elevation, which would become small islands within the swamp during high-water levels. These areas would afford the deer a highly protected environment against predators.

With my theory I began making plans to do some serious swamp hunting. I enlisted a close friend to help me transport a small boat to the swamp. With the boat I could now explore the areas where I thought the deer were concentrated. The first area on my agenda was where I felt the big 12 pointer resided. With the aid of the topo map and the boat, I located a small island. The island was located approximately 200 yards from where I had spotted the monarch.

Rowing to the island was an exciting experience. The excitement was generated when a small herd of deer suddenly bolted from the island into the water. I knew instantly I had uncovered one of the mysteries of hunting swamp deer. I also knew I had gotten a brief glimpse of a large rack before it disappeared beyond the island.

Upon reaching the island, I realized the markings on the trees were not what I had first thought. As with numerous other trees, the lower portions were void of bark. This is common in swamplands due to beaver activity, but what I was looking at was the result of large antlers scraping the trees. In other words, buck rubs were everywhere. Excitedly, I returned to my original position to hunt for the remainder of the afternoon. Time was running out as archery season was in its final days.

The following morning would be the final morning to hunt, due to school work. This weighed heavy on my mind as I rowed through the darkness toward the island. If all went well, I would be waiting in ambush when the deer returned for their daily bedding. The chill of autumn was refreshing as I watched the sun appear in the eastern sky. Nestled in my makeshift blind of cane, I waited with high expectations for what was about to occur. Nothing would distract me from the small clearing in the center of the island. I would allow nothing to defeat me if the charge arrived. These were my thoughts until I was suddenly disrupted.

The disruption resulted from the faint sound of splashing water, which grew louder with each beat of my heart. Listening to the sound grow louder, I knew my dream was about to become reality. Within seconds the deer would be on the island and my chance would be at hand. Quickly the sound of splashing water was transformed into the sound of crunching leaves that had fallen from the many small water oaks native to the island. It would be the leaves that would betray the position of the deer.

In seconds my ears detected the exact location of four deer: one on my right side, two on my left, and one directly in front of me. The leaves also informed me the deer were approaching slowly and it was time to prepare for the shot. Then suddenly the sight of the deer on my right sent a surge of excitement through me. The antlers of the seven point buck were clearly visible as two small trees shielded his shoulder. From the

Hunting the many islands located within the swamp can be the key to success.

corner of my eye I detected movement. I could now see the two deer on my left emerge. Both of these were does browsing on the ground. I could only wait to see if the fourth and final deer was my dream buck.

In the few seconds it took for the final deer to appear, my hands began to quiver with excitement. But at the sight of a four pointer my emotions sagged. Only for a brief moment did I allow the disappointment to affect

Trophy bucks such as this are not uncommon on swampland islands.

my concentration. I was sure my count was correct and I had a choice: Wait and hope the monarch would appear, or try for the seven pointer.

The seven pointer was standing perfectly broadside to me. Nothing was between us but air. In short time, my arrow had penetrated the buck. Upon the arrow's release, havoc spread throughout the island. The sound of startled deer scurrying into the water was nearly deafening.

Knowing my ears would be the vital instruments to recovering my trophy, I listened closely. The sound of splashing water faded quickly as the animals departed. Within seconds, silence filled the swamp.

With the final sounds reaching my ears I hurried to the boat. Quickly I removed the camouflage cover and headed for the other end of the island. Time was against me and I knew it. I had little time to locate the path the deer had traveled, and where I would find my buck.

In less than a half-hour, I discovered my buck. He lay only inches beneath the muddy water the deer had created while escaping. It was this muddy path I knew I must follow or it would dissolve quickly if I waited.

Since the morning I collected my first swamp buck, many more have fallen. There is no question some of the best trophies I have harvested have come from swamps. In hunting these areas, I have learned many things pertaining to hunting the magnificent white-tailed deer. The greatest of all these lessons is to never underestimate what a deer can and will do.

I have seen deer swim across large bodies of water with ease. I have seen numerous deer avoid swimming small patches of water by walking over a beaver dam instead, the largest deer of which was a splendid 11 pointer. This buck's antlers are now part of my collection. I was waiting for him on the other side of the dam with a Model 700 Remington chambered for .35 Whelen. The buck had been seen by hunters miles away feeding in a cornfield a week earlier. So what is the moral of the story?

Swamps are areas that receive little, if any, hunting pressure. During periods of high hunting pressure, swamps can become potential hot spots. This is true for hunting big, mature bucks. But it will be the hunter who knows the swamp and the ways of the deer who will harvest the gray ghost of the cyprus.

Chapter 18

Archery for Southern Deer

Bill Bynum

Hunting with archery equipment has always fascinated me. Even as a lad the ol' stick and string was a passion. There was simply something about the primitive weapon that intrigued me. The thought of knowing it would be my skill that would determine the outcome of the shot excited me.

The skill I refer to was my ability to shoot the bow instinctively. Today I still rely on this same ability for shooting my bow. I have remained an instinctive bow shooter for a number of reasons, which I will discuss later in the chapter. Some readers may disagree with my way of hunting, but this is good. All hunters have different ideas about archery equipment and bow hunting. This is one of the privileges all hunters have.

Unlike the days of my youth, modern hunters have a smorgasbord of equipment from which to select. Today hunters have better bows, arrows, broadheads, and accessories than ever before. These advancements have enabled hunters to become more efficient and harvest more deer. Without question, this is what has helped in creating the modern bow hunter. Most of the advancements have come from the experiences of dedicated bow hunters who love their sport and strive to make it better.

Archery is one of the oldest forms of hunting known to man. Bow hunting dates back to primitive man and the early days of the Bible. Most of us can relate to the bow and arrow through the American Indians. Indians relied on the bow and arrow for self-preservation. It was not until the introduction of firearms did the popularity of archery decline. But even with this decline, archery remained a form of hunting for some people.

Pioneers Of Modern Bow Hunting

A part of adolescence is having heroes. I know much of my youth was formed around my heroes–heroes whose names haunted my thoughts daily and every time I went afield. The names Pope and Young are credited with being the fathers of bow hunting, and this I cannot argue. But the names Fred Bear, Ben Pearson, and Tom Jennings echoed in my youthful mind. These were some of the men who laid the foundation for

214

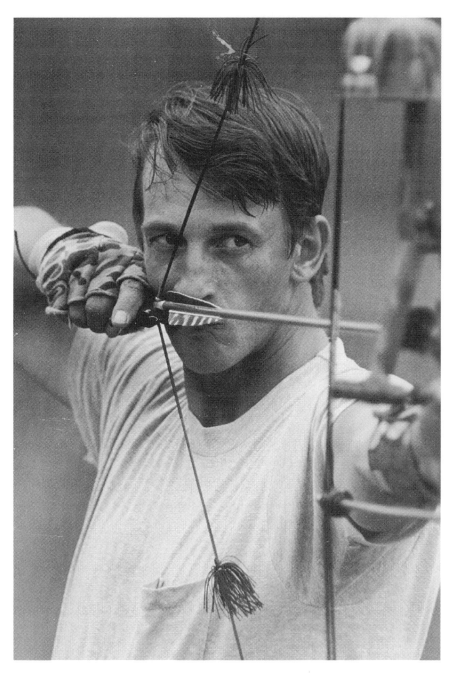

Learning to shoot a bow instinctively requires both concentration and practice from the hunter.

Bucks such as this one are what bow hunting dreams are made of!

modern bow hunting. They are names I feel all bow hunters should know. It is these names that have formed the empire of today that we all enjoy.

The first factory-made bow I ever owned was a Ben Pearson fiberglass longbow. In my youthful eyes this was state-of-the-art equipment. My grandmother sold several dozen eggs to generate the money for the bow. If memory serves me, the bow and three cedar arrows cost her about eight dollars.

With this bow and three cedar-shaft arrows, I ventured afield almost daily. Hunting anything allowable was my primary objective when I left the house. If the season was open, small game was the preferred target. Cottontail rabbits, raccoons, opossums, and squirrels feeding on the ground were stalked. If the season closed, a length of string was attached to the arrow and bullfrogs and fish were harassed. White-tailed deer did not exist, or were not huntable at this time in my life. It would be several years before the white-tailed deer would flourish in my native land of west Tennessee.

Years passed quickly while I practiced for the day I would hunt the mighty white-tailed deer. During those years I hunted and read about the exploits of Fred Bear, John Wootters, and Jim Dougherty. It would be these men who would inspire my quest for deer. It was also these men who influenced my present career.

Bill Bynum lived a dream being able to hunt with the legendary John Wootters. John poses with the results of that hunt. That's Bill's deer on the right!

The First Whitetail

The first year the state of Tennessee allowed bow hunting for deer escapes my memory. I do remember I had upgraded my bow and was carrying a Bear brand recurve bow. The new state-of-the-art aluminum arrows had dramatically increased my proficiency with the bow. My level of confidence was high and I knew I was ready to encounter a white-tailed deer.

The moment of truth came on the second day of the hunting season. In the early morning sunlight a large doe appeared from nowhere. The sight of the doe caused me to begin shaking. Trying hard to recover from the excitement, I began drawing the bow. The task quickly became a chore before I gained full draw and released the arrow. The moment I had waited for now transpired with the airborne arrow.

My eyes followed the arrow's path as I was launched into total shock. Instantly I knew my shot was high and failure was upon me. The deer responded by quickly vacating the area and performing some vocalization. With each snort of the deer I felt the agony of defeat even more.

Soon I was brought back to reality as I replayed the events in my mind. For many minutes I tried to analyze what I had done wrong and why. Little did I know that this would prove to be one of the greatest hunting lessons I would ever receive.

Bill Bynum learned early the importance of releasing every time like it was being aimed at a trophy buck.

Bill Bynum believes any deer harvested with a bow is a trophy, and only the hunter has the right to decide what is a trophy!

Another question that should be asked is, "What bow do I enjoy shooting the most?" Though this may appear to be a trick question, it is not. In most cases we will practice more with a bow we enjoy shooting. This, in turn, should lead to becoming a better shot with the selected bow.

Many hunters are discovering how bow sights increase their accuracy. Today there are many different types of bow sights available. But even with sights, accuracy is gained from shooting concentration! Concentrating on the target and the mechanics of shooting is the key to accuracy. This is true for those who shoot instinctively. Instinctive shooters know their natural shooting ability will determine the degree of accuracy achieved. This is the reason instinctive bow shooters practice regularly with their equipment. Whether the bow is a longbow, recurve, or compound, the shooter must concentrate at all times.

The All Important Arrow

When I began bow hunting, wooden arrows were about it. This did not matter as only longbows and recurve bows were available. The compound bow had not yet made its debut. So bow hunters made good use of what was available. Today, arrow shafts are constructed from wood, aluminum, or carbon graphite. In most cases, hunters will select either aluminum or graphite. Wooden shafts are not recommended for modern compound bows. In my opinion, these innovations have helped make bow hunting a much better sport. These arrows are designed to achieve maximum performance when used properly. Hunters following the manufacturers' recommendations will have few, if any, problems from these arrows. This is the reason it is important to follow all instructions and recommendations when selecting arrows.

Selecting the type of arrow to be used for hunting is a personal preference. Many hunters prefer aluminum over carbon graphite and vice versa. Some hunters prefer the lightest possible arrow weight to achieve arrow speed. These hunters feel the faster an arrow travels, the better! This is why some people use an over-draw system for hunting. The over-draw system allows shorter length arrows to be used in the bow. The shorter arrow weighs less and will achieve greater speed than longer, heavier arrows. In the minds of some hunters this is the key to harvesting game, but not mine!

In my opinion, the most important factor for the arrow is to contain energy. The arrow should contain enough energy to penetrate to maximum levels. This energy is influenced by both the arrow's speed and weight. This is the reason all arrow/broadhead combinations should be tested for maximum penetration before going afield. It is the *duty* of every hunter to utilize the best in penetration performance.

Without question, the degree of penetration is a subject of debate. Some hunters prefer for the broadhead to remain inside the animal. These hunters believe that, with the broadhead remaining inside more damage is being done. This belief is based on the broadhead cutting

A combination of both arrow weight and speed is needed to penetrate big bucks such as this one.

while the animal is moving about. While there may be substantial evidence for this belief, I prefer maximum penetration.

Maximum penetration in my words is *complete* penetration! Complete penetration ensures eating venison. When complete penetration is achieved, more tissue is damaged or cut. The more severe the cut the higher the rate of blood loss within the animal, and the more the animal hemorrhages the quicker death will occur. With complete broadhead penetration, there will be two wound openings. This will allow more blood to escape from the animal for easier recovery.

Now the tricky part: How do you achieve complete penetration? I wish I could say I have a formula for complete penetration all the time. But there are too many factors pertaining to complete penetration: arrow speed, arrow weight, distance of target, you name it and it will influence the degree of penetration.

To achieve complete penetration, some important factors must be applied by the hunter. One such factor is the *draw weight* of the bow. The draw weight of the bow will determine the speed of the arrow upon being released. The speed of the arrow will also be a determining factor in the amount of energy the arrow will have upon impact. In short, the more energy, the better the arrow/broadhead combination can perform. This is the reason hunters should use the maximum draw weight that is comfortable. The combination I refer to is arrow weight and broadhead

Complete penetration is a must for ethical bow hunting, according to Bill Bynum.

performance. As we have already reviewed arrow weight, I will explain broadhead performance.

Making The Point

Without question, there have been heated debates over broadheads. Some hunters swear by two-bladed broadheads while others swear at them. Again, this is a matter of personal preference. What is important is that the broadhead performs its primary duties, which are to fly correctly, perform maximum penetration, and maximum cut. Without all three duties being performed, negative results can be expected.

In most cases, proper broadhead flight will be obtained when the blades of the broadhead are aligned with the fletch of the arrow. Though this may be the general rule of thumb, it is not always correct. Often I have to make several adjustments before good flight is achieved. I have also encountered broadheads that simply would not tune properly. This is the reason that I have a large box of assorted broadheads in storage.

An important factor in broadhead performance is sharpness. This is a factor some hunters may take for granted. Many hunters think a broadhead is razor sharp just because it is new. Sorry, this is not always true. In fact, I have discovered few broadheads from the package are near their full potential for sharpness. Razor sharpness can be obtained with a couple of strokes on an extra-fine honing stone. This is true even with detachable insert blades offered on today's market.

Every broadhead should be checked for maximum sharpness.

Southern deer are not quite as large as their northern relatives, but they are still fun to hunt!

Dealing With Dixie Deer

Throughout this book I have expressed my opinions pertaining to various aspects of southern deer hunting. One thing I have not expressed myself on is the deer in general. Southern deer are somewhat different than their northern relatives. In general, deer located in the southern states are smaller in body weight than northern deer. Also, most hunters will discover the antler size of southern deer to be smaller. Of course, there are some splendid bucks scattered around in some areas. Every once in a while a nice buck is taken from the common (public) hunting grounds. But for the most part, the really good bucks of the South will be located in management areas.

In recent years, deer management programs have become influential to southern hunting. With these programs, the quality of southern deer is becoming better. Today hunters can find excellent trophy opportunities throughout the South. This is why it is important for visiting hunters to research the area they will be hunting.

Locating good hunting can be accomplished by contacting a state's wildlife agency for information. It is always good to know the number of deer within the area and the harvest record. The southern states have a lot of deer. Most southern states allow archery hunters more than enough time to harvest their share. So all and all, the sunny South can be a bow hunter's dream.

Chapter 19: Part I

Guns for Southern Deer: Rifles

Bill Bynum

During the past three decades I have fired lead from an assortment of rifles. I have owned rifles of various actions chambered for various cartridges. With these rifles I have harvested scores of deer all across the country.

I have witnessed some deer drop at the crack of the gun, and some not! In most cases, the negative results were due to poor bullet place-

The sight of a big buck can cause some hunters to become excited.

ment. Therefore, the best rifle to hunt with is the rifle with which you are the most accurate.

Maybe my last statement sounds a little strong, but a fact is a fact. Many hunters today are miserable marksmen and blame the gun. True, there are various factors that can and will influence the outcome of a shot, but in most cases you will discover it was simply poor marksmanship.

Some hunters take marksmanship for granted. What I mean is that they do not practice under actual hunting conditions, or they do not practice at all. Practice is one of the most important factors in being an ethical hunter. It is every sportsman's obligation to be as efficient with the rifle as possible. This means being able to place the bullet exactly where you want, when the time arrives.

Bench Or Buck

Over the years I have observed some pretty funny things while hunting. I have seen hunters miss deer standing still at ten yards, and hit two-inch targets at 100 yards. Was this due to the rifle? I don't think so! More than likely, it was due to several of the following reasons.

One would be *hunter excitement*. In many cases the sight of deer sends electrical surges through a hunter. The sight of a really nice buck can have a negative impact on the human nervous system. Hunters begin to breathe hard and perform erratic body movements (shaking) like never before. So what is the key? Simple, try to remain calm during the shot. Get excited after you have placed the harvest tag on the deer, not before.

Learning to remain calm is a lot easier said than done, I know, but the more one is around deer, the more accustomed one becomes to deer. If you have trouble controlling yourself, I suggest spending time in the woods observing deer!

Practicing from a bench is an important factor in becoming a good marksman. From bench rest positions we learn how our rifle is performing. Bench rest shooting allows us to practice under non-stressful conditions. This is important and one of the first stages to becoming a good marksman.

Today hunters have a smorgasbord of rifles and cartridges from which to select. In most cases any of today's popular deer cartridges will quickly dispatch deer. With the exception of the .22 caliber centerfire cartridges, all centerfire cartridges are good choices. The reason .22 centerfire cartridges (.222 Rem., .223 Rem., 22/250 Rem.) are not suitable is their overall performance on big game. There is no question these cartridges are capable of killing a white-tailed deer; the question is whether or not most hunters are capable of placing the bullet properly within the animal. From my experiences with most hunters, they are not! With that said, let's move on to the common cartridges for deer.

In selecting a cartridge for southern deer the issue of recoil is important. In most cases, recoil will be expressed by the shooter as the *kick* of the gun. Often recoil results in pain or unpleasantness for the shooter.

This often creates a syndrome I refer to as "recoil conscious." Most of the time the person experiencing this syndrome will be a woman or a youngster. This is the reason I list deer cartridges in three categories. The categories are: mild, medium, and heavy recoil.

Mild Mannered Cartridges

I receive a lot of mail asking what cartridge I think is good for recoil-conscious hunters. Without question, the two cartridges that head the list are the .30-30 Winchester and the .257 Roberts. Both of these cartridges are more than capable of collecting deer within their yardage limitations. This is due to the amount of foot pounds of energy the bullet will sustain upon striking the animal. This energy will determine the amount of damage the shot area will receive. It will be the amount of damage that determines the outcome of the shot.

The .30-30 Winchester

The .30-30 Winchester cartridge is, without question, one of the most famous cartridges ever known to man. The .30-30 Winchester cartridge

The .30-30 Winchester cartridge is popular among lever action rifles.

was first chambered for the Winchester Model 94 lever action rifle in the year 1895. Both the rifle and the cartridge have experienced a long life in the shooting world. The cartridge name (.30-30) implies that it was originally a black powder load, a .30 caliber bullet loaded with over 30 grains of black powder. The original load existed for only a short time, as this was the time in history when most loads were being transferred to smokeless propellants.

Perhaps one of the reasons for the success of the .30-30 Winchester is due to its popularity among deer hunters. With 100 years behind it, this cartridge still ranks among the top deer cartridges of today. The reason for this can be attributed to a number of things.

One of the best reasons for the success of the .30-30 is that it is chambered in some of the less expensive rifles offered on today's market. Both the Winchester Model 94 and the Marlin Model 336 are chambered

The .257 Roberts cartridge is an excellent deer cartridge for hunting heavy cover.

for this cartridge. Both are lever action rifles and are sound investments for the deer hunter.

The .257 Roberts

Sadly there are some cartridges that receive little, if any, glory. In comparison to many of today's popular cartridges, the .257 is just such an underrated cartridge. The .257, in any of its versions, is an excellent deer cartridge. The most popular of the versions are the .257 Roberts, the .257 Roberts Improved, and .257 Weatherby Magnum.

The original design of the .257 was nothing more than a 7 X 57 Mauser case necked down to receive a .25 caliber bullet. Roberts proudly named his creation the ".257 Roberts."

After a few years of being labeled a "wildcat" cartridge, Remington made the cartridge a commercial load. With only a few alterations in the case design, the cartridge was chambered for the Remington Model 30 rifle. Soon, other rifles were receiving the chambering as other companies also saw the potential for the new cartridge. Within a matter of years, the .257 Roberts was a well-known cartridge, and justly so.

The appealing factor of the .257 Roberts was its versatility. Due to its trajectory, the Roberts was a highly effective varmint rifle. The .257 Roberts had no trouble propelling 60- and 75-grain bullets at muzzle

=== TRAJECTORY CALCULATION ===

LOAD 2 DESC: .257 Roberts
ZERO RANGE: 100

TRAJECTORY UNITS: yards

RANGE yards	1) WGT: 100 BC:0.304 SH: 1.50				2) WGT: 100 BC:0.388 SH: 1.50			
	PATH	VEL	ENRGY	TOF	PATH	VEL	ENRGY	TOF
0	-1.50	2800	1741	0.0000	-1.50	2800	1741	0.0000
50	-0.12	2650	1559	0.0562	-0.14	2682	1597	0.0559
100	0.00	2504	1392	0.1150	0.00	2567	1463	0.1136
150	-1.27	2364	1240	0.1768	-1.19	2455	1338	0.1737
200	-4.08	2228	1102	0.2421	-3.83	2345	1221	0.2364
250	-8.65	2096	975	0.3115	-8.04	2239	1113	0.3020
300	-15.21	1969	861	0.3854	-14.00	2135	1012	0.3707

velocities of over 3,600 plus feet per second. The heavier 100- to 120-grain bullets left the barrel traveling at over 2,600 or more feet per second.

These loads proved to be effective on deer-sized animals. In fact, many hunters would consider the .257 Roberts adequate for caribou and black bear. This is a feat many hunters would not consider for the cartridge that stunted the popularity of the .257 Roberts, the .243 Winchester!

In comparison, the .257 not only shoots flatter than the .243, but also retains its energy better! Amazing how some gun writers of the past could have so much influence over the public. I am not saying the .243

229

Winchester is a bad cartridge, I am simply saying that I think the Roberts deserves better than it receives.

Next in line are what I refer to as the medium recoil cartridges. In all respects, these are possibly the most popular of the deer cartridges. In most cases these cartridges will handle almost any southern shooting condition. The unique thing about this category is it actually belongs to one cartridge, the .308 Winchester.

The .308 Winchester

Perhaps one of the most overlooked cartridges of today's top deer cartridges is the .308 Winchester. Though this cartridge has been around for decades, many hunters fail to use it. The reason for this could be that the .308 Winchester does not receive the press given to the other, popular cartridges. But don't think for a second that this is not one heck of a working cartridge for the serious hunter. In a nutshell, the .308 Winchester is one of the most versatile and efficient cartridges of our time. The .308 has been chambered in every feasible rifle action known.

It has also been the cartridge that has inspired some of today's popular cartridges such as the .243 Winchester and the 7mm/08 Remington cartridges. Perhaps the reason for this is the remarkable accuracy the .308 provides the shooter. From bench rest shooting to big game hunting, the .308 has proven to be one of the most accurate cartridges ever known.

Two of the first rifles to be chambered for the .308 were the Winchester Model 70 bolt action and the Winchester Model 88 lever action. The year was 1952 when these rifles were offered to the shooting public. At first shooters responded negatively to the .308 because they felt that the popular .30/06 Springfield could do anything the .308 could do, and do it better. When using the .308, hunters should research their ammunition for the best loads possible for dispatching the animal.

The factors I look for in load performance are how much energy the bullet will transfer upon striking the animal and how the bullet will perform. The .308 Winchester is capable of transferring excellent energy levels at the common ranges of deer shooting; therefore, the emphasis should be placed on the type bullet selected for the .308.

Having shot a fair number of deer with this cartridge through the years, I can say few animals ever left their tracks after the over-the-counter Winchester 180-grain Power Points reached them. Some of my hunting buddies like to use 150-grain bullets that expand rapidly. They feel the higher velocities and fast expansion of the bullets are more lethal. After seeing dozens of whitetails receive both load types, I cannot force myself to speak badly of this cartridge. I can also see why my friends like their loads, as they have never lost an animal when the .308 was used.

In my opinion, cartridge selection is a personal matter. Ethical hunters know what they can and cannot do. In most cases southern hunters prefer cartridges that will quickly dispatch a deer. Cartridges such as

Bill Bynum has used the .308 Winchester for many years and feels it is an excellent choice for hunting deer-sized animals.

This fine Texas buck was taken on the Nail Ranch with a Ruger Number One rifle chambered for .30-06 Springfield.

the .30-06 Springfield and those derived from the .30-06 do just that. Cartridges such as this are developed for improving the overall performance of the parent cartridge. One such improvement is the .280 Remington.

The .280 Remington

Time has also allowed the modern deer hunter a wide selection of the so-called "perfect cartridges." This term is usually used with the "perfect deer rifle," which usually revolves around a specific cartridge or load. Therefore, we are now a society of perfect hunters as we now have the perfect firearms and ammunition, right? Sorry, I don't think so.

If we were a society of "perfects" we would never miss our shots. We would never wound an animal or commit any of the errors that make us human. Let's forget about the word "perfect" and concentrate on the words "good" and "adequate." The reasoning for my choice of words is this: If the hunter performs good marksmanship with an adequate cartridge, venison will be on the menu.

Today there are numerous cartridges that are more than adequate for hunting deer. Some of these cartridges have been around for decades due to their popularity. There are also some excellent cartridges that do not receive much mention. Until recently, the .280 Remington was one of these cartridges. Perhaps this was due to Remington changing the cartridge's name to the 7mm Express Remington. Maybe it was due to hunt-

Bill Bynum believes the .280 Remington is one of the premier deer cartridges of our times.

ers learning how effective this cartridge was and did not care what some said about it.

History shows the .280 Remington was first introduced in 1957. This was 32 years after the introduction of the ever-famous .270 Winchester. This could be one of the reasons the .280 had a slow start. Also, the .280 was first introduced in the Remington Model 740 autoloader. Autoloaders were not the most popular rifle actions of that time period, either. The dominators of the media preferred bolt action rifles, yet another strike against the .280 Remington.

In reality, the .280 Remington is close to being nothing more than the .30-06 Springfield necked down to take the 7mm bullet. Like the .270 Winchester, which is also a .30-06 necked down, another comparison is needed. The comparison is accuracy. From my observations of comparing the two cartridges on the range, the .280 wins again. The testing was done with various factory ammunition at 150 yards. The five shot groups from both rifles and all ammo were within a two-inch diameter. The best grouping came from the .280. From my Model 700 Remington, all groups could have been easily covered with a quarter.

Today, as never before, hunters should perform their tasks more cleanly and ethically. This is why I feel it is important that hunters understand the ballistic factors of their equipment.

Perhaps I have not been as technical as some may have liked, but what I want to emphasize is that I think the .280 Remington is one of the finest hunting cartridges ever developed. I also think it is a cartridge that deserves a lot more praise from the media than it has received in

The bolt-action is a top choice among all professional hunters, such as Craig Baddington.

the past and present. In my opinion, the .280 Remington is a working cartridge for the working hunter.

Over the years I have been privileged to harvest many deer across North America. In doing so I have used just about every cartridge known for deer hunting. These cartridges that have been reviewed are only a few of the many fine cartridges available. The type of rifles these cartridges chamber into can be quickly summarized.

The type of action the rifle has is a personal decision of the hunter. The type of sights, brand name, or any other factor pertaining to the firearm is the hunter's personal choice. All I can do is urge each and every hunter to stand up for their personal rights! Without each and every one coming forth and defending our Constitutional rights, this chapter will become nothing more than a memory in history!

Chapter 19: Part II

Muzzleloaders & Handguns

Larry L. Weishuhn

Muzzleloaders

I like to hear a loud "bang" when I shoot at a southern whitetail–or any other whitetail for that matter! I am a confirmed rifle and handgun hunter. While I find bow hunting great fun, it is not really my cup of tea. I have, however, taken several deer with a bow and in time will attempt to take some more, primarily because of the early and liberal seasons. Bow hunters have an advantage when it comes to white-tailed deer hunting seasons. They get to hunt before rifle hunters and they generally get to hunt much longer. The modern bow hunters, through their lobbying efforts, did an excellent job of selling the various wildlife departments on archery seasons.

Throughout this book I have made reference to various rifles and cartridges. Those who have hunted with me and have attended my hunting seminars know I favor the .280 Remington and several of the other 7mm cartridges. Although I am not particularly a fan of the various magnums, I have hunted with them and used them to take animals, but I tend to prefer the standard cartridges. In most instances we hunters tend to shoot them more accurately than we do the magnums.

My esteemed co-author, Bill Bynum, is a bow hunter, but one who also hunts with rifles and handguns, as well as with muzzleloading rifles. It seems appropriate that my first whitetail hunt with Bill was a muzzle-loader hunt in his home state of Tennessee.

The first white settlers in the South armed themselves with muzzle-loading rifles, primarily flintlocks. These settlers with their rifles protected themselves and their families from those who did not wish them to be there. They also used their firearms to shoot a wide variety of game animals and birds to feed their families and also their friends and neighbors. Those early muzzleloading rifles and pistols were not always accurate or reliable, even though many southerners gained reputations far and wide as marksmen.

236

Larry Weishuhn with a Georgia buck taken with a .50 caliber, Thompson/Center Treehawk.

With the introduction of the caplock rifles, reliability and accuracy seemed to increase. Early hunters were reputed to be able to shoot the eye out of a squirrel at phenomenal distances. Rather than shoot a squirrel in the head (considered a delicacy by some), they "barked" the squirrel by shooting right next to the squirrel's head, sending bark from the tree on a deadly mission. Having tried this many times with both modern and primitive arms, I am not too sure of this method of taking squirrels.

Muzzleloaders On The Rebound

During the last few years we have seen a resurgence of interest in muzzleloading rifles. Today we also have rifles and handguns that are capable of extreme accuracy, thanks to modern technology and the use of new bullets and plastic sabots designed for barrels with the appropriate twists.

To some extent I consider myself a traditionalist. Standing next to the fireplace in our home are several fine black powder rifles. They are the half-stock style of the Hawken. A couple of others are typical Pennsylvania long rifles. All have fancy wood, shiny patch boxes, and are truly a beautiful sight to behold. I have hunted with them in the past. Now they are primarily for show.

As a traditionalist I occasionally put on my old buckskins, strap on my fancy powder horn, and stand in front of the mirror or step outside for photographs. Then as quickly as I am finished, all those things go back in the closet. I have no desire to tramp around in the woods wearing buckskins, shoes that may be comfortable but are also always wet and cold, and carry a rifle I am not sure will fire when I pull the trigger. The only reason the early mountain man and hunter did not use a modern muzzleloader, with Pyrodex, a telescopic sight, modern bullets with sabots, and wear new high tech clothing is simply because they did not have them. That's the only reason, pure and simple. As I stated, it is fun to dress as a traditionalist, but I am afraid I have become addicted to the modern times. Even though a lot of hunters might not admit it, I suspect they feel the same way.

In recent years we have seen the addition of special black powder or muzzleloading seasons throughout the South. These seasons allow us opportunities not previously available. When and where possible, I try to take advantage of those situations, as do many other hunters.

In selecting a muzzleloader rifle, choose one that fits and suits you. There are many available from companies such as: Thompson/Center, Modern Muzzle Loading, White Muzzle Loading Systems, CVA, Dixie Gun Works, Traditions, and many others. All produce excellent rifles, including the popular in-line systems that assure the rifles will "make smoke."

It is my opinion deer hunters should use no less than .50 caliber rifles. They should also use bullets designed for deer. While the true traditional black powder shooters might prefer patched round balls, I will opt for various maxi-balls and modern bullets cased in plastic sabots. These are much more accurate, in general, and are also more accurate at long distances.

Bill Bynum with a Modern Muzzle Loading MK-85, .50 caliber topped with a Simmons variable scope. The only reason the early day mountain man did not use this type of gun and equipment is because it was not available.

David Hale with a monstrous buck taken with a Modern Muzzle Loading MK-85.

Favorite Blackpowder Rifles

The two black powder rifles I find myself using more than others are the Modern Muzzle Loading MK-85, .50 caliber, in its Predator Model and a Thompson/Center Thunderhawk in a .54 caliber. I opted for the .54 over the .50 caliber in the Thunderhawk, because if the occasion ever arises, I intend to use it for moose and elk. Both are now scoped with variables. Scopes are legal in Texas. In other states I have to remove them and use iron or peep sights because the use of telescopic scopes is not legal in some states. Be sure to contact the game departments in the states you intend to hunt before doing so with a scoped rifle. These laws are changing quickly from state to state. Giving such information here would likely be worthless.

Using modern bullets with a sabot I have taken deer out to 200 yards with the MK-85. I suspect I will be able to do the same with Thunderhawk. I have shot it at those distances, but not at game.

Rather than give specifics as to proper loads of Pyrodex or black powder and bullets, I would strongly suggest getting in touch with the various muzzleloader companies, or at least the one that manufactured the rifle you have or are interested in purchasing. These companies can give you specific bullet and load recommendations for their guns.

Hunting with a muzzleloader is little different than hunting with a modern rifle or shotgun. The techniques used are the same as when hunting with a modern rifle or bow.

I once made a statement that the only way I would again start shooting a black powder rifle was when I was rich enough to use a barrel a few times, then throw it away and get a new one so I would not have to clean it. Alas, I have once again started hunting with muzzleloader rifles and handguns. Using Pyrodex and many of the new synthetic lubricants and cleansing agents makes muzzleloading a lot less labor intensive than it once was. It also makes muzzleloader hunting less messy. However, it is still wise to run a wet patch through the rifle after each shot. Modern black powder rifles have come a long way in a relatively short period of time. With the addition of the many new primitive arms hunting seasons, the future has never been "blacker." In this case that means brighter!

Handguns

I once interviewed an old-time Texas sheriff who shot a Boone and Crockett whitetail with his .45 Long Colt handgun while he was on the track of a fugitive from the law. When I asked him about the deer and the hunt, he was quick to reply that he shot the deer with the handgun because it was the only gun he had at the time. To quote him, 'I'da shot that buck with any kind of gun. He was the best buck I had ever seen in nearly 60 years of kicking around the Brush Country. I shot him with my handgun, an old .45 Long Colt Peacemaker because I didn't have anything else!'

The Revolver Cartridges

Throughout my hunting career I have hunted with handguns. I have had other guns with which to hunt so I have not had to rely entirely on a handgun such as the old sheriff. I have used handguns primarily because I enjoy hunting with them. Perhaps I was influenced by watching cowboy movies when I was growing up in the 1950s and early 1960s.

Like many handgun hunters, I started by shooting a .22 revolver, then quickly switched to larger caliber revolvers, single-shots, and even semi-autos. During my early days of hunting deer with handguns I used an old .45 ACP, Remington Model 1911. It was accurate out to about 50 yards. With this gun I took my first whitetail, a doe. I quickly graduated to various .357 Magnums, a .45 Long Colt, a .41 Magnum, and eventually several .44 Magnums. When the Thompson/Center first introduced its Contender single-shot handgun, I purchased a .30-30 Winchester. For many years I hunted with that Contender taking a variety of game, including several whitetails. Along the way I also picked up a Remington XP-100 chambered for the .35 Remington.

Since the mid-1980s I have handgun hunted almost exclusively with various .44 Remington Magnum revolvers and the many Contenders

Handgun hunting is becoming increasingly popular throughout the South. While taxidermist Tom Hicks prepares to shoot, Larry Weishuhn watches.

chambered for rifle cartridges as well as wildcat Contender cartridges such as the 6.5 JDJ, .309 JDJ (my confessed favorite), and the .375 JDJ.

Since the days of the "Dirty Harry" movies there has been a lot of hype about how powerful the .44 Magnum is. In truth it is a good handgun cartridge, but it has its limitations. In discussing rifle cartridges I believe a round should no longer be considered adequate for whitetail at that point or range where it no longer produces at least 1,000 foot pounds of energy. To put the .44 Mag handgun cartridge in proper perspective, most all .44 Magnum loads produce no more than 600 foot pounds of energy at the muzzle! The venerable .30-30 Winchester produces well over 1,000 foot-pounds of energy at beyond 100 yards. Does this lack of downrange energy disqualify the .44 Remington Magnum handgun as a deer cartridge? No, but it does make it a round that requires the shooter to use precise shot placement and to know his limitations at making a killing shot. In my opinion this lack of downrange energy makes the .44 Mag handgun one that should not be shot at deer beyond the distance of 75 yards.

You will likely have noticed that I have not mentioned the .357 Mag cartridge. This round, in my opinion, is marginal when it comes to the handgun deer cartridges. While there are those who tout the merits of this round, it is at best an expert's hunting gun. If you wish to hunt with a revolver, much better choices of cartridges are the .41 Rem Mag, the .45 Long Colt, as mentioned the .44 Rem Mag, or the .454 Casull.

A New Idea Is Formed

I have hunted with a great variety of .44 Rem Mag revolvers, including the Ruger Super Redhawk, the Ruger Super Blackhawk Hunter (as well as other Ruger Blackhawks), Wesson's Model 744, various Smith & Wessons, and Colt Anacondas. In the case of the Colt Anaconda, I had an opportunity to work with the people from Colt in developing a new innovative package.

Allow me to digress just a bit. Most revolvers are available in either stainless steel or blued steel. Both are rather shiny and bright. While I like the non-corrosive and rust-deterrent quality of stainless–both important in southern climates–I do not care for the bright color. In the deer woods stainless steel handguns shine like a beacon on a dark night. The same is true for rifles. But generally when you are hunting with a rifle you have long-range capabilities and opportunities at deer. With a handgun, and especially a .44 Mag revolver, you normally have deer at close range. Remember, I said I thought it should not be used on deer at beyond 75 yards. When deer are close, they are going to see you moving your revolver into a shooting position. For that reason I can see where it is important to use either a handgun with a dark non-glare or non-shiny finish or one that is totally covered with camouflage.

Moving out of the South for just a moment, it was while hunting on the famed Sanctuary in Michigan that the guys from Colt, David Richards and Robert Silinski as well as Skipper Bettis, who runs the Sanctuary, and I came up with the idea for a new Colt Anaconda Hunter Package. While filming with David Blanton of "Realtree Outdoors," we noticed deer immediately picked up any movements I made with my handgun. Thus we camouflaged my handgun and scope using a Realtree adhesive tape. Thereafter I could move the handgun slowly and get away with all kinds of movement. Out of necessity a new idea was born.

The new Anaconda Hunter or Sanctuary Package will consist of a Simmons variable handgun scope, mounts, and an Anaconda handgun totally camouflaged in Realtree's All Purpose Gray. The process by which the camo pattern is applied makes it virtually impossible to chip or scratch it off. I have tried. The new handgun combination will allow you and your handgun to simply disappear in the woods. While I hunted several times with the new Colt camoed handgun, I have not yet hunted with it nearly as much as I intend to.

I have used a variety of .44 Mag ammunition, from the various quick expandable bullets to hard cast bullets. Two loads I have used quite a bit on deer are the 240 grain PMC Eldorado Starfire and Randy Garrett's 310 grain hard cast loads. I have shot several deer with the former. Individual handguns are like rifles--each gun shoots different loads differently. In the handguns I use, I have had success with the loads mentioned as far as accuracy and terminal bullet performance on deer are concerned. There are other good loads produced by Win-

Larry Weishuhn with a decent Texas Hill Country buck taken with a .44 Remington Magnum revolver.

chester, Remington, and Federal, as well as others and numerous handloads.

Thompson/Center Contenders

If I had to choose one handgun with which to hunt it would undoubtedly be the Thompson/Center Contender. I own several with a variety of barrels. As to a favorite in the readily available commercial Contender line, it would be the .375 Winchester in a Super 14-inch barrel. Were I allowed the luxury of a barrel in another caliber, or a wildcat cartridge, it would be the .309 JDJ, hands down! Both of these are capable of quickly bringing down deer at ranges near and far, especially the .309 JDJ. Using 150 grain Nosler Ballistic Tip handloads I have shot numerous groups at the bench of less than an inch at 100 yards, and 2-1/2-inch groups at 300 yards. I have taken several deer with the .309 JDJ at ranges out to beyond 150 yards. The .309 JDJ is a .444 Marlin case necked down to a .308 caliber. It was developed by J.D. Jones of SSK Industries in Wintersville, Ohio.

The .375 Winchester was first introduced in a Winchester Model 94 Big Bore rifle. Thompson/Center added it to its lineup of Contender cartridges some time later. Normally I shoot Winchester commercial loads using 200 grain bullets and have taken several deer. The round is accurate and hard hitting, especially in the Contender. While it does have some recoil, it is certainly not objectionable.

Scoped handguns, such as Weishuhn's scoped .309 JDJ T/C Contender, are extremely accurate. Ron Porter takes a convenient rest and prepares to shoot at a distant deer.

Larry Weishuhn with a good non-typical buck taken with his .309 JDJ Contender handgun.

Other good southern deer cartridges available in the Contender include: the 7-30 Waters, .30-30 Winchester, .35 Remington, and .45-70 Government. Quite often these rounds perform better in the Contender handguns than they do in the rifles they were designed for.

There are also several other good hunting handguns such as those produced by Magnum Research. Its handguns are available in a variety of rifle cartridges. My only experience thus far with its Lone Eagle has been with one chambered for the .308 Winchester. That one shot great. I am anxious to try the Lone Eagle in the woods.

For years I occasionally hunted with a Remington XP-100 chambered for the .35 Remington. With it I took several southern deer, the best being a big, wide typical 11 point I shot for ESPN's "North American Outdoors" television show filmed in Texas. The XP-100 is a fine hunting handgun. But, while attending the 1995 Shooting, Hunting and Outdoor Trades Show, I learned Remington plans to discontinue the handgun.

Because of diminishing eyesight I can no longer clearly see iron or open sights. For that reason and a multitude of others (including being able to make more precise shot placement), I now exclusively shoot revolvers and single-shot hunting guns topped with handgun scopes. Most of my current handguns wear Simmons 2.5 to 7X variables. I like the variables because they allow me greater versatility in shooting at ranges near and far. They also help me pick out a spot through which to place a bullet when hunting in thick brush, which is so often the case when hunting southern deer.

Practice, Practice And More Practice

The key to becoming a good handgun shot is practice! Practice, practice, and more practice. Learn the capabilities of the handgun and the cartridge you choose at ranges near and far, but then also learn your own capabilities with your handgun at those same ranges.

Although I shoot handguns often, I make it a matter of protocol not to shoot at any deer unless I first have a solid rest. If I hunt from a tree stand or tripod, I make sure it is one that allows me to get a solid rest before I shoot at an animal. If I am still-hunting, I spend half my time looking for deer and the other half of my time looking for something against which I can get a solid rest. I also carry a set of crossed shooting sticks, occasionally commercial models, other times simply two fairly straight and stout sticks I cut for the purpose of using them for crossed-sticks shooting rests.

Hunting with a handgun for big whitetails excites me. So do big whitetails. Thus, when I finally do get a shot at a good deer I want to eliminate as many things that can go wrong as possible. Solid rests and shooting sticks help me do just that.

Handgun hunting is growing throughout the South. I for one could not be any happier!

Chapter 20

Southern Deer Management, Looking to the Future

Larry L. Weishuhn

There is change in the air. Southerners are awakening to quality deer management! Revolutionary deer management ideas and practices that started in South Texas in the 1970s through the efforts of wildlife biologists Al Brothers, Murphy E. Ray, Jr., Bob Zaiglin, this writer, and a few others, are finally spreading throughout the "Old South," and doing so like a wildfire. In the South the early flames were lit and fanned by J. Wayne Fears when he introduced and initiated quality deer management techniques and programs on properties owned by Westervelt Lodge and forest lands administered by the lodge's parent company. To many southern hunters these were revolutionary ideas. Later college professors and researchers such as Dr. Larry Marchinton, Dr. Harry Jacobson, Dr. James Kroll, and wildlife biologist Joe Hamilton picked up the torch and have continued spreading the word. Through their efforts and many others, an organization was begun to promote quality deer management throughout North America, but especially in the South. The organization is known as the Quality Deer Management Association. The new organization is serving as a rallying point for those who wish to discuss and promote the proper management of white-tailed deer and their habitat.

Quality deer management should be a grass roots movement initiated by hunters and landowners alike. The movement without the cooperation of only one of the "factions" can cause problems in any efforts toward properly managing deer.

Since the early 1970s I have worked with landowners and hunting groups throughout the whitetail's range. In each instance it was at their request that I met with them and viewed their property before we set up a management program on the properties they owned or hunted. Thankfully we received considerable cooperation from the state's wildlife or

Quality deer are no accident, they must be planned and managed!

game department. In some instances it took several years to get the land-owner or group to go along with all my recommendations.

Planting "Seeds"

As a biologist involved in quality deer management programs I "planted seeds," and then let them grow and mature. That way it seemed to those involved, the ideas "they came up with" were their own. The end product was worth the wait!

Deer management in the South is changing. There are several reasons for this. Hunters have seen what management programs can do in other areas to increase antler development and body sizes. The overall age of hunters is increasing as well. With maturity, hunters generally become more interested in the quality of the hunt and the animals they hunt and take. With age, less emphasis is placed on how many bucks were taken each fall and more on the size or age of the deer taken. The change is a slow one. If I have led you to believe the change is rapid, then I have led you astray. Old traditions die hard.

Deer management involves not only people and deer, but involves habitat as well. Quite frankly the "wellness" of the habitat determines what wildlife is present and to a great extent how it fares. Wildlife populations, especially white-tailed deer, have great reproductive capabilities. They can recover much faster than the habitat where they live.

Deer management programs are most often measured by the quality of bucks within a deer herd. This quality is dependent upon age, nutrition, and genetics. In most areas of the South, whitetails have excellent genetic potential. The deer in the South are basically a melting pot of deer from throughout North America. The result is a great gene pool. But genetics is also the one factor controlling deer quality over which we have the least control. While there are harvest schemes that we can employ to alter genetics, the effects are still minimal compared to the other two factors over which we have considerably more control. Those two factors are something we as hunters and managers can readily do something about to greatly improve deer quality.

Beginning Changes

One of the easiest things we as hunters can do to improve the quality of the local deer herd it to pass up young bucks and allow them to mature. White-tailed bucks generally do not start producing their best antlers until they are at least three years of age. Up until that time they are trying to grow both body and antlers, and body development is always going to take precedence over antler development. Once the buck's body matures, any nutrition not needed for maintenance can be channeled into antler development. Quite simply that is why mature deer produce better antlers than do younger bucks. Research tells us some bucks have their best antlers during their fifth or sixth year. However, I have seen many bucks produce their best antlers, by far, after they were beyond that age. Having worked with a lot of different deer herds and penned deer operations, I am convinced bucks continue producing big antlers until they have reached an advanced age, as long as they have more than adequate nutrition throughout their life. Several bucks on properties I managed had their best antlers when they were between eight and 10 years of age, and still had huge antlers when they were 13 years old. Managing for such old deer is impractical. However, it can happen!

Nutrition is another factor over which we as hunters and managers can have tremendous control. To produce big bodies and antlers, whitetails should receive a daily diet of 16 percent or higher protein, in the presence of vitamins, minerals, and carbohydrates from the time they are born and throughout life.

To increase the nutritional level there are several things we as hunters and managers can do. The first is to properly harvest both sexes, bucks and does, to bring the total herd into the forage production capabilities of the habitat. We can also plant various forages to increase the food supply and its quality throughout the year, especially during the stress periods of late summer and late winter. Additionally we can, where legal, establish salt and mineral licks, or even use supplemental feed. We can also fertilize native deer browse species. All these are merely tools we can use to increase or improve the nutritional intake of deer. They are not all encmpassing answers or "purple panaceas" or remedies to the question of quality deer management by themselves.

In most any white-tailed deer management program, at least as many does as bucks should be harvested annually.

Planting supplemental forages can help increase the nutritional intake of whitetails.

Goals And Objectives

Age, nutrition, and genetics are all simply pieces of a large puzzle. Other ingredients include people and their commitment; time (most quality management programs take at least three years before you can expect to see results); as well as soil types, vegetation types, agricultural and silvicultural practices, and climatic conditions.

The first step in setting up a quality deer management program is to determine long-range goals and objectives. Without objectives the management program can have no direction. In many of the management programs I have been involved with, our goal has been to produce a deer herd where we maintain the adult and total deer density at a certain number or density; where the buck to doe ratio will be no less than one buck per two does; the buck herd will be comprised of at least 40 percent mature bucks over the age of four years; and the mature deer will gross score a minimum of 140 Boone and Crockett points. We also occasionally set a minimum goal for field-dressed weight.

After long-term goals and objectives have been decided, the next step is conducting a census to determine the deer density, as well as the buck to doe ratio and the fawn survival rate. From these data responsible harvest decisions and recommendations can be made.

Taking census of southern deer herds is no easy chore. Because of dense woods and the overstory, this is sometimes a nearly impossible task. If you have any questions about how to conduct a deer survey in your immediate area, contact your local wildlife biologist or game warden. Chances are excellent the local state game officials are already doing a game survey in your immediate area and can provide you with special insight about what is there.

After determining what is on the property, you can decide how to make responsible harvest recommendations relative to your long-term goals and your fawn survival rate. The future of the deer herd is dependent to a great extent upon the number of fawns produced and reared each year. On most of the properties I manage we always take at least as many does as we do bucks. The numbers of bucks we harvest annually depends on the total number of bucks on the property, the current and goal buck to doe ratio, the average age of bucks present, and the fawn survival rate. The same is true when it comes to harvesting does.

If for several years only bucks have been harvested, and no does, it may be necessary to reverse the harvest for at least a couple of years. This is not only to allow more bucks to enter the population, but to allow those there to get a year or two older.

Which bucks to harvest is dependent upon many factors. The point I elude to is whether or not to harvest spikes. Suffice it to say there is sufficient research to support the taking of spikes, if you are interested in producing the finest bucks possible. There is also research that shows spikes eventually develop good racks. What to do?

Taking census of whitetails, where possible, is one of the first steps to determining harvest recommendations.

The ultimate decision about deer management is made by you, the hunter!

What To Do With Spikes

On some properties I manage or oversee, we harvest every spike we see. On those properties we are trying to produce only a few, but also the finest antlered bucks possible. On other properties we do not shoot any spikes. The decision on what to do about spikes depends entirely upon your long-term goals and the current deer population. However, it must be said regardless of what you decide about harvesting spikes, harvesting spikes alone will not create a quality deer herd!

The future of white-tailed deer management in the South is exciting! The southern lands have great potential for producing quality deer herds and especially big white-tailed bucks. The South has excellent soils, and receives timely and sufficient amounts of rainfall to produce forage crops ideal for producing big bodies and antlers. Winters are relatively mild and winter-kills are normally not a problem. The South has great potential to go well beyond what it has done thus far, relative to deer management and hunting. The ultimate decision as to the track it will take and the extent to which deer management will be practiced is entirely dependent upon you, the hunter. You are the ultimate deer manager!

Zero in on successful deer hunting with these four exciting new books!

WHITETAIL: THE ULTIMATE CHALLENGE
by Charles J. Alsheimer
6"x9", softcover, 228 pg., 150 photos
Learn deer hunting's most intriguing secrets from America's premier authority on using decoys, scents and calls to bag a

buck. Find insight on the whitetail's rut cycles, where and how to hunt whitetails across North America, rubs, scrapes, the impact of weather conditions and much more! Plus, many spectacular black and white photos.

Available June 1995

$14⁹⁵

HUNTING MATURE BUCKS
by Larry Weishuhn
6"x9", softcover, 256 pg., 80 photos
Learn how to take those big, smart, elusive bucks. Excellent blend of scientific knowledge and old-fashioned "how-to" gives you the information you need. Also learn behind the scenes management techniques that help balance doe/buck ratios to produce bragging-size whitetails.

Available February 1995

$14⁹⁵

AGGRESSIVE WHITETAIL HUNTING
by Greg Miller
6"x9", paperback, 208 pg., 80 photos
Learn how to hunt trophy bucks in public forests and farmlands from one of America's foremost hunters.

"Hunter's hunter" Greg Miller puts his years of practical experience into easy-to-understand advice that will help both bow and gun hunters bag that trophy. Ideal for busy outdoorsmen that have neither the time nor finances to hunt exotic locales.

$14⁹⁵

Available February 1995

SOUTHERN DEER & DEER HUNTING
by Bill Bynum and Larry Weishuhn

These two popular southern hunters and DEER & DEER HUNTING field editors join forces to bring you the history of deer in the south, plus techniques that work below the Mason Dixon line as well as anywhere whitetails are found. Understand terrain, firearms, equipment, rattling and calling along with much more firsthand experience that's guaranteed to bring you success in southern climates.

Available June 1995

$14⁹⁵

ORDER TODAY! BUY ALL FOUR BOOKS AND GET FREE SHIPPING!*

Please send me:

____ copy(ies) WHITETAIL: THE ULTIMATE CHALLENGE...$14.95 $ _____

____ copy(ies) HUNTING MATURE BUCKS...$14.95 $ _____

____ copy(ies) AGGRESSIVE WHITETAIL HUNTING...$14.95 $ _____

____ copy(ies) SOUTHERN DEER & DEER HUNTING...$00.00 $ _____

Shipping ($2.50 for first book, $1.50 for each additional book, FREE if you buy all four) $ _____

WI residents add 5.5% sales tax $ _____

Total Amount Enclosed $ _____

Name _____

Address _____

City _____

State _____ Zip _____

❏ Check or money order (to Krause Publications)
❏ MasterCard ❏ VISA

Credit Card No. _____

Expires: Mo. _____ Yr. _____

Signature _____

Mail with payment to:
KRAUSE PUBLICATIONS
Book Dept.WDB2, 700 E. State St., Iola, WI 54990-0001

*Books shipped upon publication

For faster service MasterCard and VISA customers dial toll-free
800-258-0929 Dept.WDB2
6:30 am - 8:00 pm, Sat. 8:00 am - 2:00 pm, CT